Sewing
SCRAP BLOCKS
with Character

Sewing Scrap Blocks with Character

Landauer Publishing, *www.landauerpub.com*, is an imprint of
Fox Chapel Publishing Company, Inc.

Project Team
Editorial Director: Kerry Bogert
Editor: Amy Deputato
Copy Editor: Hayley DeBerard
Designer: Mary Ann Kahn

ISBN 978-1-947163-42-3

Library of Congress Control Number: 2020024435

We are always looking for talented authors. To submit an idea, please send a brief inquiry to
acquisitions@foxchapelpublishing.com.

Note to Professional Copy Services:
The publisher grants you permission to make up to six copies of any quilt patterns in this
book for any customer who purchased this book and states the copies are for personal use.

Printed in Singapore
23 22 21   2 4 6 8 10 9 7 5 3

This book has been published with the intent to provide accurate and authoritative
information in regard to the subject matter within. While every precaution has been
taken in the preparation of this book, the author and publisher expressly disclaim
any responsibility for any errors, omissions, or adverse effects arising from the use or
application of the information contained herein.

Sewing
SCRAP BLOCKS
with Character

Olesya Lebedenko

Contents

Introduction

Hello, fellow crafters! This book celebrates my year-long challenge. It was May 1, 2018, when I decided to start the 365 Days of Quilt Scraps Challenge (*#365daysquiltscraps*) and sew one block per day for a whole year. The step-by-step tutorials presented here are based on blocks that I made during this challenge. I created them to show some fun and easy ways to use your scrap fabric. You can see more of these blocks at my Instagram account, *@olesyalebedenkodesign*.

I think that all makers and crafters (I'm a quilter and doll maker) have an innate ability to collect fabric scraps. I seem to be incredibly talented at this—between my classes, my workshops, and my own projects, I have scraps everywhere in my two-story shop! But most of us don't know how to use all this treasure. The blocks in this book demonstrate the technique of combining small scraps of fabric to sew an endless variety of designs.

During my year-long challenge, I was inspired by everything around me: my family, books, animals, cartoons, and even the aroma of a morning cup of coffee. When creating blocks from sketches, I used a pencil, a ruler, and transfer paper to map out pattern designs. Once I finish a pattern, I love mixing my fabrics. I stand in front of the fabric stash on my shelves and choose the right fabric for each element of the design. After putting all the pieces together, it's decoration time! I'm a big fan of different techniques, including drawing, stitching, appliqué, and embroidery. It's amazing how tiny fabric pieces can come alive with a few decorative touches!

I believe that the characters featured in this book will inspire you to use your wealth of scrap fabric to create and sew quilt blocks. Join the blocks together into a quilt or use them in other projects.

Be inspired! Keep sewing!

—Olesya Lebedenko

Useful Tools and Materials

Here's what you will need to create the projects in this book:
- Your amazing fabric scraps! Pieces of all sizes and shapes will be perfect for the blocks in this book.
- Patterns, transfer paper, and pencil or water-soluble marker. You can find all patterns at the end of the book.
- Sewing needles, thread in different colors, and pins
- Sharp scissors
- Ruler and rotary cutter
- Tiny buttons, beads, and cross-stitch thread in different colors for decorative touches
- Embossing tools (1.2mm and 1.8mm) for characters' eyes
- Paintbrush for face details
- Textile paint in black (or dark brown), white, and red for detail work
- Water-based pigment ink pad (I recommend a rose color) for blush on faces

How to Use This Book

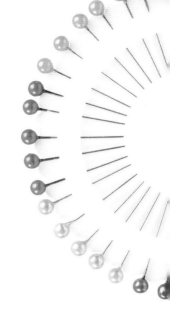

About the Blocks

This book offers quilters a cornucopia of original patchwork block designs based on my *#365daysquiltscraps* year-long challenge. I've included easy-to-use gridded templates for enlarging the designs and piecing. You can trace full-size templates from the page or cut ready-to-use transfer-paper templates so you can start sewing immediately.

All of the blocks in this book are created with basic patchwork sewing; I made many of them with a combination of machine stitching and hand stitching. I recommend machine sewing when the pieces are approximately 1¼" (3cm) or larger, and hand stitching with anything smaller. You can enlarge and adapt the patterns for paper piecing if desired.

Some of the blocks are decorated with painted, appliquéd, or embroidered details. Add all details once you've pieced the block together. If you plan to do machine quilting, sew on any beads and buttons after quilting.

Each block design includes a full-size photo and pattern (excluding seam allowances) and diagrams with step-by-step sewing instructions to construct the block. The finished size for most blocks is 3½" square (9cm square). *Note: When printing or copying a pattern, choose "actual size" or "100%." It's a good idea to make a practice block at larger than 100% before you try the patterns at actual size.*

To make a block, cut out all the pattern pieces and then sew the pieces together following the steps shown in the diagram. The numbers indicate the correct order in which to sew the pieces.

Always sew with a ¼" (0.6cm) seam allowance, keeping in mind that the templates *do not* include the seam allowance. Sew the pieces together from edge to edge, unless otherwise noted, and backstitch at both the beginning and end of each seam (if hand-sewing, make knots). The yellow and red dots indicate when to start and stop sewing, respectively, at the seam allowance, rather than sewing from edge to edge. This technique is used to set pieces into each other.

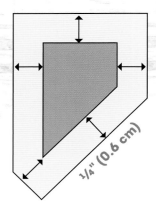

The templates *do not* include seam allowance. When cutting your fabric, add a ¼" (0.6cm) seam allowance around each piece.

Cutting the Blocks

All of the patterns in this book are shown at full size; you can enlarge or reduce them as desired. Each pattern is printed on a grid with measurements in inches and centimeters. Use these measurements as your starting point when resizing. For best results, use a photocopier to resize the patterns.

To prevent frayed edges and for safety while cutting, I recommend pinking shears.

Painting Details

Use textile paint to add details such as eyes and small dots and dashes. Textile paint is especially important if you want your project to be washable. For most of my blocks, I used white and either black or dark brown paint. First, mark the details (eyes, mouth, dots) with a fine-tipped water-soluble marker or ballpoint pen and then paint over your pen marks. For eyes and dots, I recommend using an embossing tool (1.2mm or 1.8mm) or the head of a small pin to apply paint.

Sewing from Edge to Edge

Example 1

Sew from edge to edge and press the seam allowance.

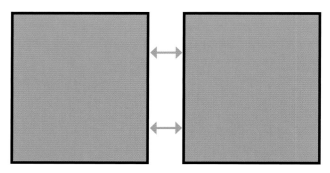

Pieces before sewing, as shown in the project steps.

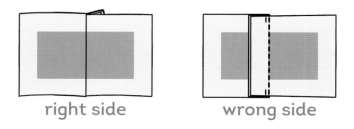

right side   wrong side

After sewing from edge to edge.

Selecting Fabrics

Many of the blocks in this book are low-volume (low-contrast) patchwork, so the block instructions do not include materials lists. Take a look at the patterns and finished blocks, and try to find everything you need in your collection of fantastic fabric scraps.

Example 2

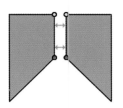 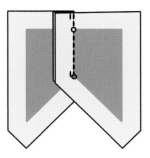

Pieces before sewing, as shown in the project steps.

After sewing (wrong side shown).

Example 3

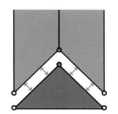 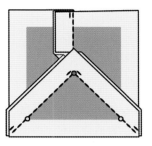

Pieces before sewing, as shown in the project steps.

After sewing (wrong side shown). Stop sewing at the red dot and press the seam allowance.
Remember, the seam allowance is not pictured in the project steps.

- Red dot = stop sewing
- Yellow dot = sew from edge to edge

How to Make Decorative Stitching
Backstitching

If a dotted line is shown on the color illustration for a project, it indicates backstitching for the block's decorative details, such as lips or a spider web. Draw the details on an already sewn block with a water-soluble marker (or chalk) and backstitch using heavyweight thread or floss. Remove any visible markings with water and a cotton swab.

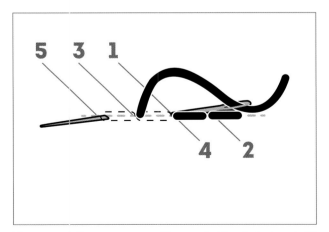 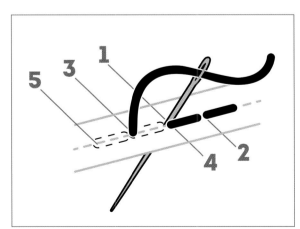

Your needle comes up through the fabric at (1) and goes down at (2). Continue along your pattern line, move a space ahead (3) and bring your needle back down into the same hole at the end of the last stitch you made.

Outline Stitching

A bold line on a template indicates the outline stitch. This is a flexible stitch that can follow gentle curves. Please pay careful attention to the following stitching instructions to make perfect lines. Note that all stitch points in the outline stitch will fall *on* the stitch line.

Draw the details on an already sewn block with a water-soluble marker (or chalk) and backstitch using heavyweight thread or floss. Remove any visible markings with water and a cotton swab.

I worked this stitch from left to right. These instructions are for right-handed quilters.

Fig. 1. Bring out the thread through (1) and take it in through (2). Take the needle backward and bring the thread out through (3). Make sure the point (3) lies under the stitch (1–2). *Note that the point (3) lies about halfway through (1) and (2).*

Fig. 2. Take the needle in through (4). Try to mark (4) in such a way that the point (2) will lie halfway through (3–4). Bring the needle out through (2). The stitch point (2) will be at the bottom of the previous stitch.

Fig. 3. Continue this pattern of stitching, with the needle always coming out from the bottom of the previous stitch. The reverse of the fabric will give you a backstitch pattern.

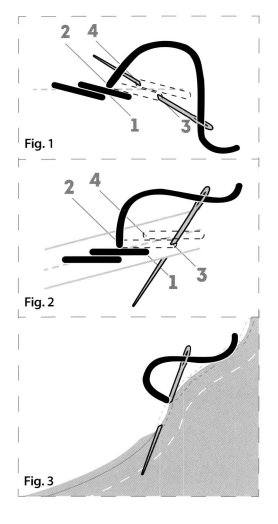

Fig. 1

Fig. 2

Fig. 3

Appliqué and Blind Stitching

You will appliqué some details, such as on faces, with blind stitching by hand (or, if you prefer, machine). To do this, cut the piece to be appliquéd, then roll the edge under and sew with blind stitches.

The appliqué technique is illustrated here in step-by-step detail, using Scary Pumpkin (see page 55) as an example.

1. Trace the appliqué design with a water-soluble marker on the right side of the main fabric.

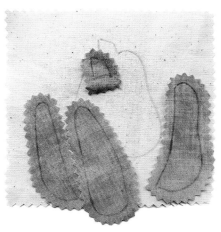

2. Trace all pieces of the design and cut them out with a ¼" (0.6cm) seam allowance.

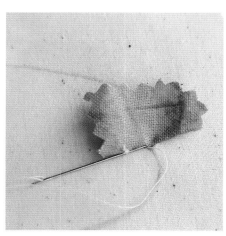

3. Use the tip of the needle to turn the seam allowance under along the marked line, then blind stitch.

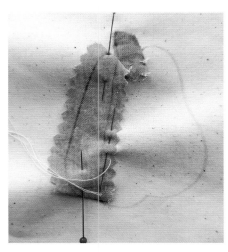

4. To appliqué a piece with the wrong side down, lay the piece in place on the background fabric and pin. One of the sides will be covered with the top part of the design, so you don't need to blind stitch. Make a running stitch along the side.

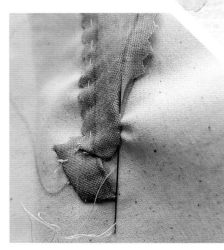

5. Use the tip of the needle to turn the seam allowance under along the marked line, then blind stitch.

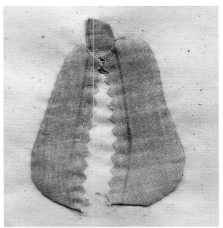

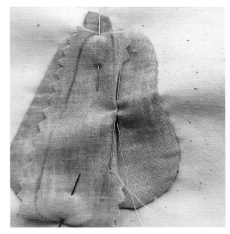

6. Appliqué the other side in the same way.

7. To complete the pumpkin, pin the middle part in place and begin to blind stitch around the piece. Follow the shape and turn the seam allowances under as you stitch.

8. Trace the face details. When working with dark fabric, I recommend using a white pastel pencil because it makes visible marks that are also easy to remove. Cut the pieces out with a ¼" (0.6cm) seam allowance. Follow the curves and be careful not to cut inside the traced lines.

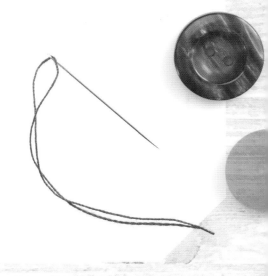

9. Lay the smile piece in place and pin. Blind stitch, following the shape and turning the seam allowances under as you stitch.

10. Applique all details of the pumpkin's face in the same way. Remove the traced line with a damp cotton swab. Iron the block.

Reverse Appliqué

Here I explain the reverse appliqué technique in step-by-step instructions, using Rabbit Silhouette (see page 61) as an example.

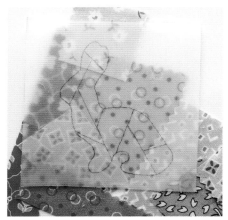

1. Select and prepare the fabrics for Rabbit Silhouette block.

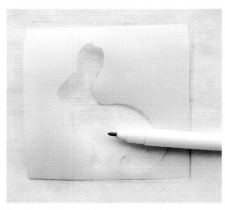

2. Cut the silhouette and transfer on the right side of the top fabric.

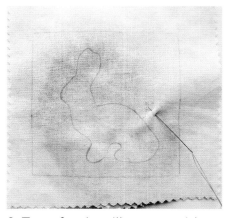

3. Transfer the silhouette with a water-soluble marker. Place the sewn block with the right side up to the back side of the top fabric. Baste with a running stitch. For easy thread removal, do not make a knot.

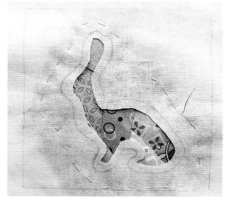

4. Carefully cut out the rabbit silhouette inside your traced line, cutting through only the top layer of the fabric. Remember to leave a ¼" (0.6cm) seam allowance.

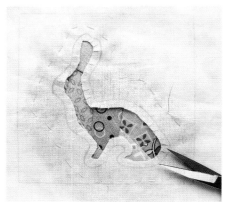

5. Clip the curves, being careful not to clip past the traced line.

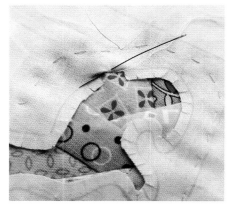

6. Turn the seam allowance under along the traced line and blind stitch.

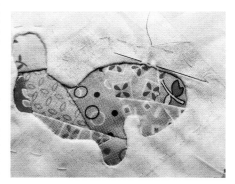

7. Make a running stitch along the edge of the silhouette.

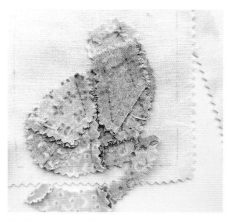

8. Cut extra fabric if needed.

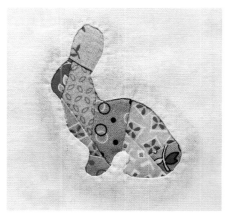

9. Take out the basting thread and use a damp cotton swab to remove the traced line. Iron the block.

Decorative Stitches, Buttons, and Beads

When I use embroidery floss, I usually divide it into six strands and use one strand for backstitching. For outline stitching (such as in Spider [page 45] and Witch on a Broom [page 46]). I used four strands to give the stitches some volume. Remember, if you plan to machine-quilt, add all beaded and button details after you have finished quilting.

The following step-by-step instructions on how to add decorative touches to your block use Aurora the Snowy Owl (page 23) as an example.

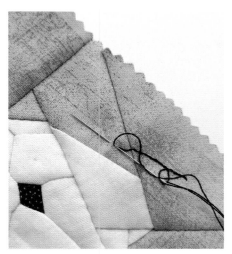

1. Draw the garland with a water-soluble marker. Divide the embroidery floss and separate one strand to use for backstitching.

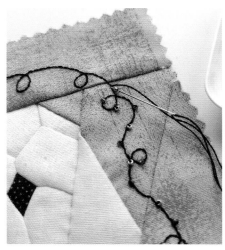

2. Sew each bead with two stitches.

3. Make a loop using one strand of the embroidery floss.

4. Secure the loop with a stitch.

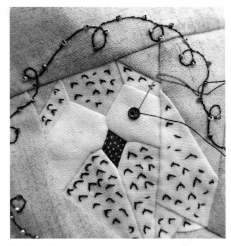

5. Decide where to place the eyes and mark each spot with a water-soluble marker. I chose tiny buttons for the eyes, attaching each one with several stitches.

6. Make stitches on the head, body, and wing to make feathers; use the same method to make the claws. Secure the loop with a stitch.

A Block from Start to Finish

All the blocks in this book are geared toward confident quilters who want to challenge themselves. To help you understand the diagrams in the projects, here is an in-depth step-by-step look at how to create a block, using Meowtie's Prize (see page 74) as an example.

1. Choose your fabrics and gather all needed tools and materials.

2. Trace the pattern onto transfer paper. I use numbers to mark my fabric, but you can use any method that makes sense to you.

3. Trace all the pattern pieces on the wrong side of the fabric.

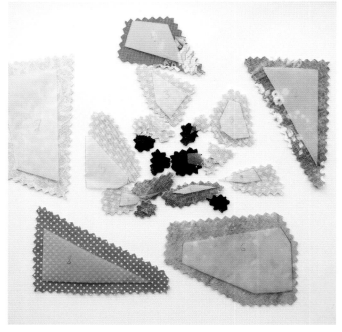

4. Transfer paper is a great tool to ensure that you cut your fabric pieces exactly as you want them.

5. Pin the pieces with the right sides facing each other and sew the first pieces together. You do not need pins for tiny pieces.

6. Using a seam-pressing tool, press firmly to get a crisp seam.

7. Pin the edges to make sewing easier as you proceed with putting the pieces together.

8. Iron the block firmly to get a crisp seam.

9. After you've put all the tiny pieces together, you can use a machine for quicker sewing. Pin the pieces and sew from edge to edge unless otherwise noted.

10. Use an embossing tool to make precise dots with white textile paint for the eyes.

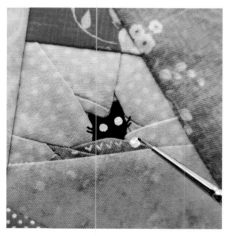

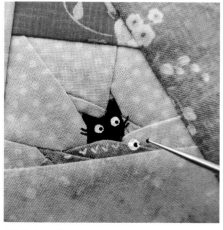

11. With a very thin brush, create the details: whiskers on the cat's face and scales on the fish.

12. Wait for the white paint to dry (drying time depends on the paint used). Make tiny black dots for the pupils with black paint.

13. The final result! The block is a combination of shapes, colors, and designs with tiny details.

PART ONE

Christmas and Winter Fun

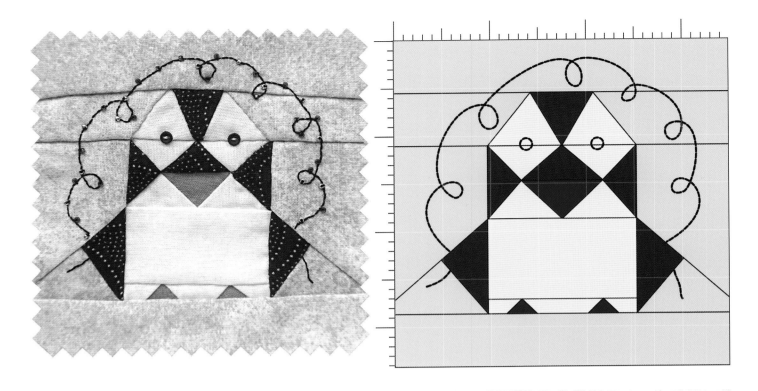

Happy Penguin

Meet this joyful penguin with a garland of Christmas lights! I used beads for decorating, but you could also use knots of different-colored threads or tiny buttons. *Pattern on page 96.*

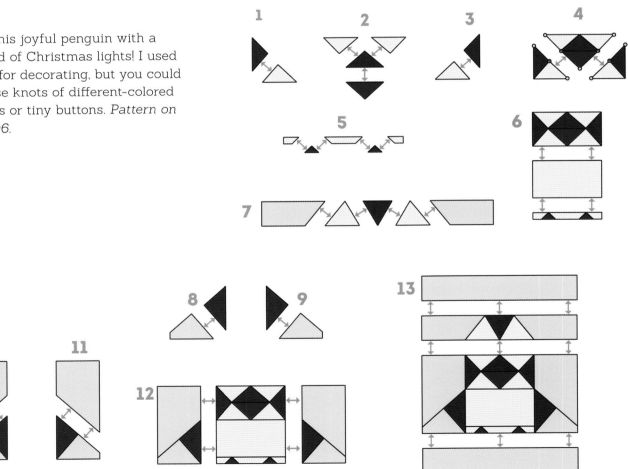

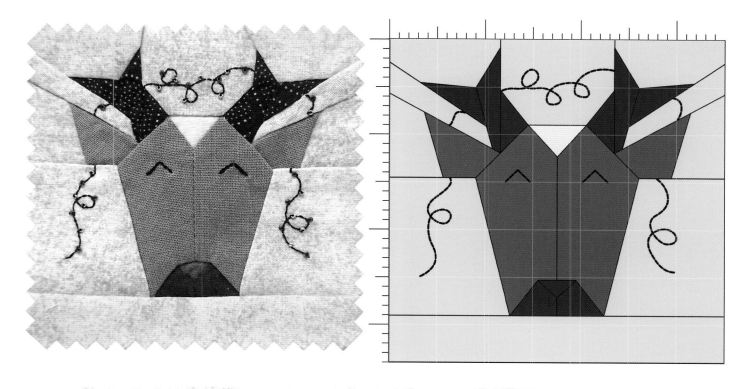

The Red-Nosed Reindeer

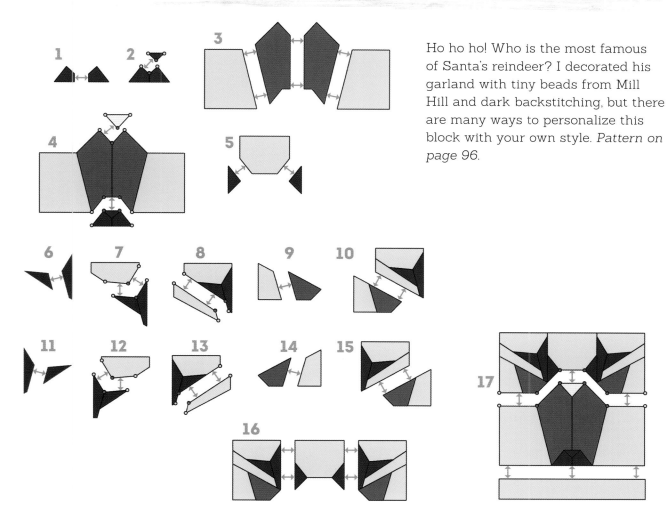

Ho ho ho! Who is the most famous of Santa's reindeer? I decorated his garland with tiny beads from Mill Hill and dark backstitching, but there are many ways to personalize this block with your own style. *Pattern on page 96.*

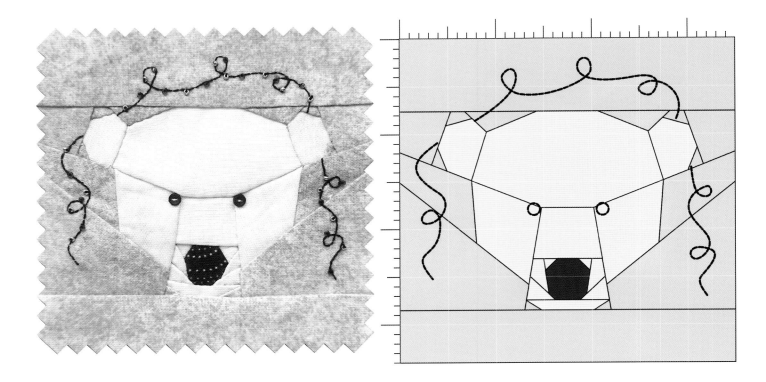

Serious Polar Bear

When I was a child, I used to watch a cartoon with a polar bear cub named Umca. This memory inspired me to design a block with a grown-up polar bear. He's a little bit serious, as all bears are, but he is really very friendly. Aside from the nose, this block is rather simple in construction. *Pattern on page 96.*

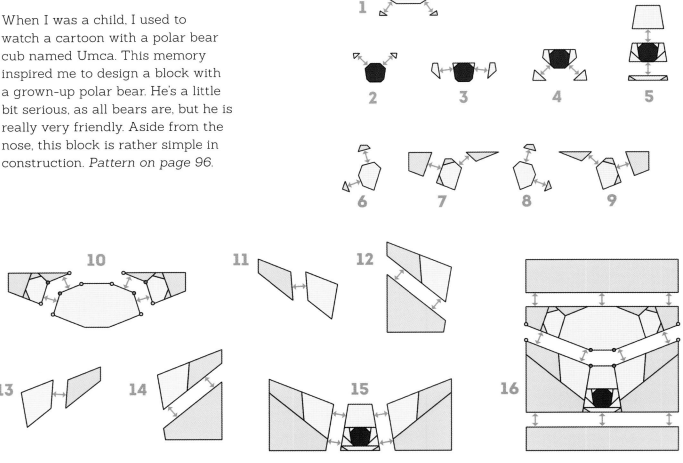

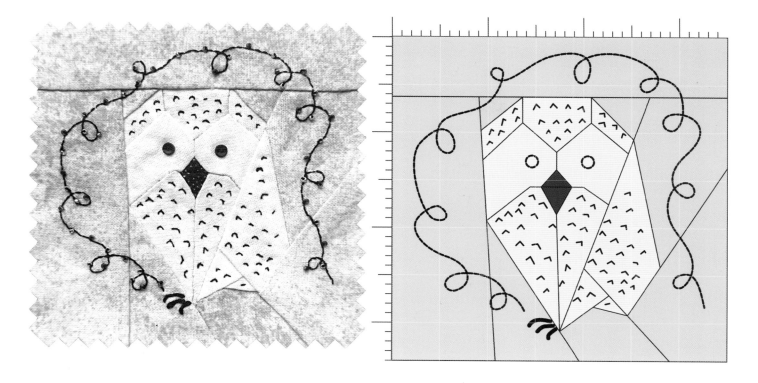

Aurora the Snowy Owl

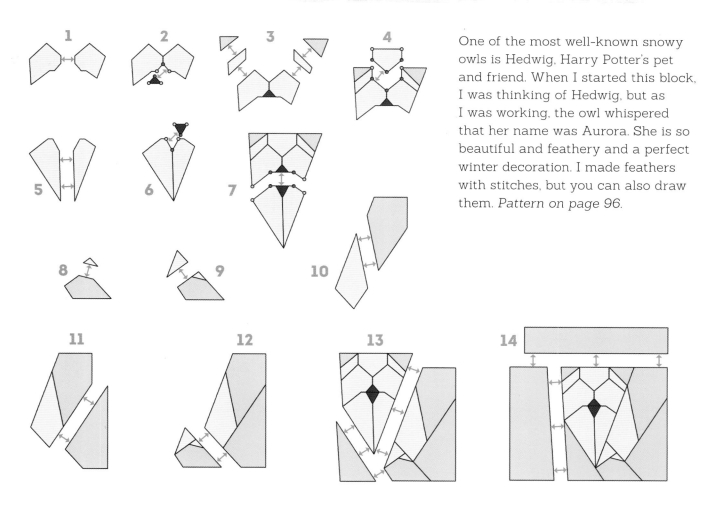

One of the most well-known snowy owls is Hedwig, Harry Potter's pet and friend. When I started this block, I was thinking of Hedwig, but as I was working, the owl whispered that her name was Aurora. She is so beautiful and feathery and a perfect winter decoration. I made feathers with stitches, but you can also draw them. *Pattern on page 96.*

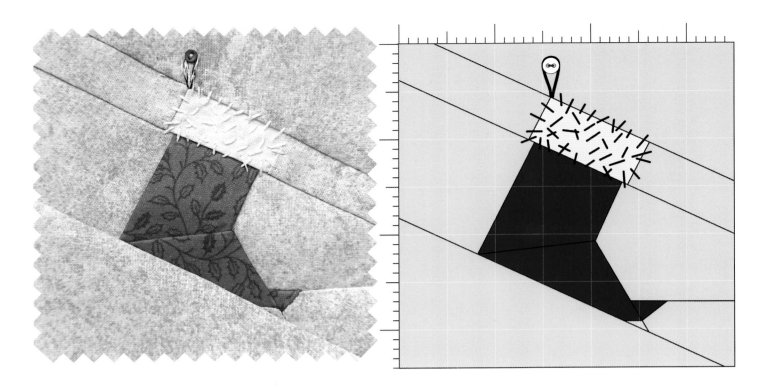

Santa's Stocking

Have you ever wondered where Santa puts his own presents? I think he puts them in a stocking! This Christmas stocking is "hanging" from a tiny button with red-and-white cord and decorated with white stitches. You could add some snowflakes or some decorative beads or knots around it. *Pattern on page 97.*

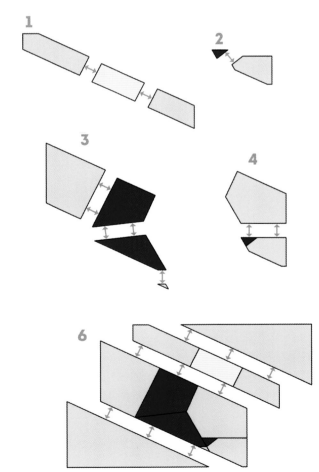

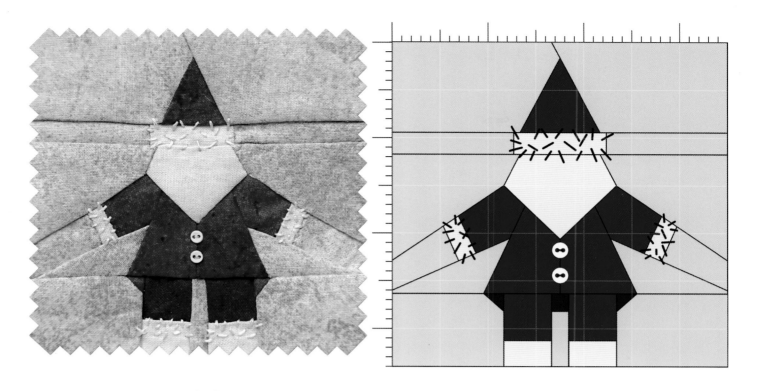

My Father's Santa Suit

In the country where I grew up, we call Santa "Father Frost." To create a holiday miracle, my dad would dress up as Father Frost—and now it's my husband's turn. In this block, I decorated Santa's suit with tiny buttons and white stitches. Stitch or draw some snowflakes for a wintry decorative touch. *Pattern on page 97.*

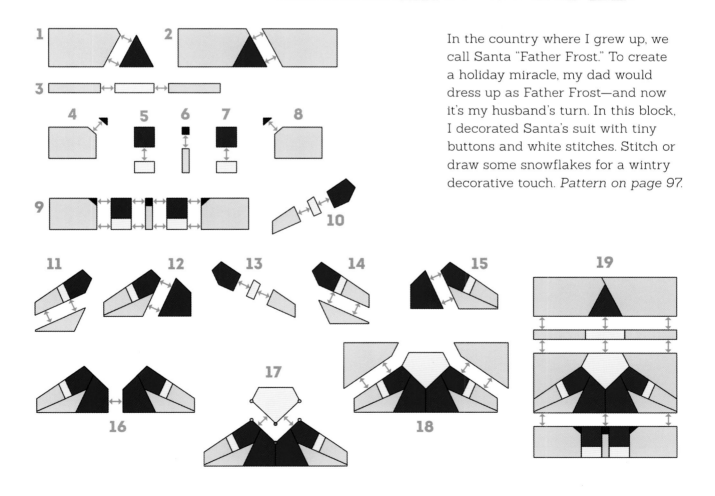

Clever Santa

This entire block is made by blind-stitching appliqué. It was a lot of fun to hand-appliqué the glasses because they are stitched in layers. Make the frame of the glasses first, as a whole piece, and then appliqué the lenses. *Pattern on page 97.*

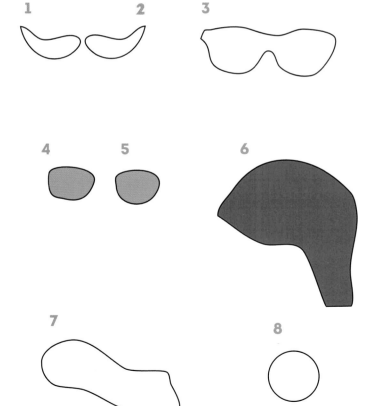

Merry Santa

Here is another block made with the blind-stitching appliqué technique. I love these small, quick projects. You can add some detail by making crazy stitches on the hat! *Pattern on page 97.*

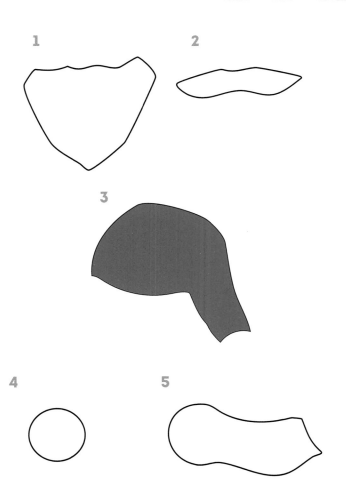

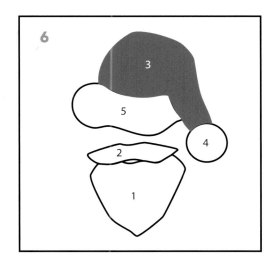

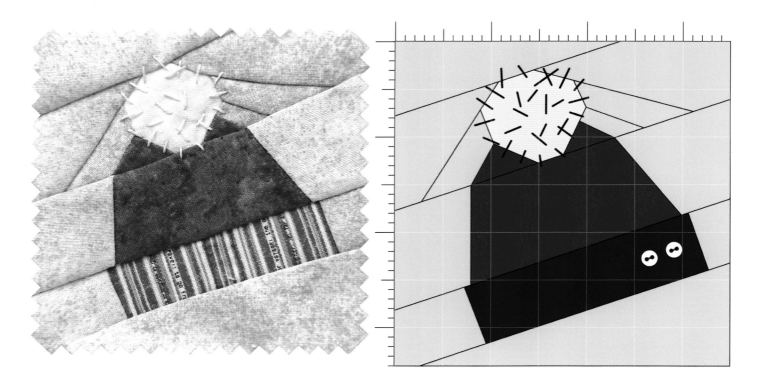

Cozy Hat

When it's freezing outside, you need a warm hat for your head. This block is very easy to sew and does not take long to complete. I used some white stitches to make the fuzzy pom-pom at the top, and you can decorate your hat with different stitches, French knots, beads, or buttons. *Pattern on page 98.*

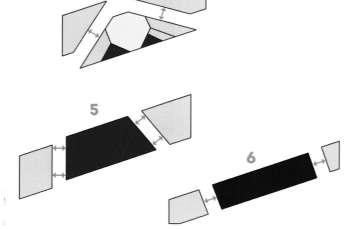

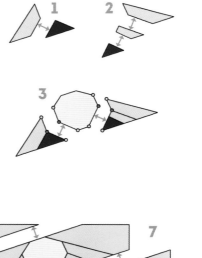

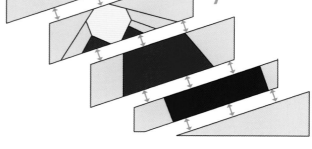

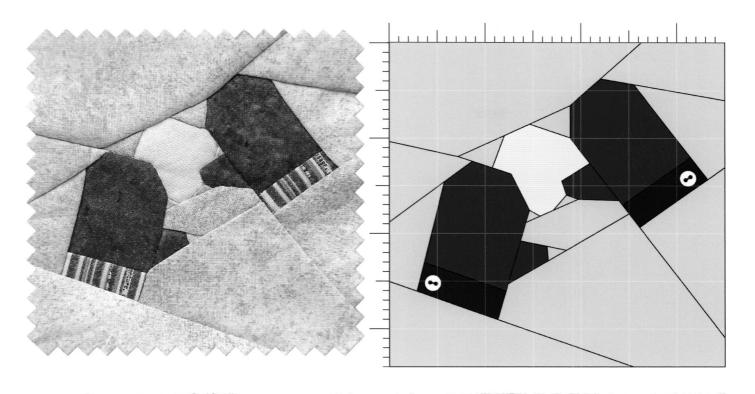

Warm Mittens

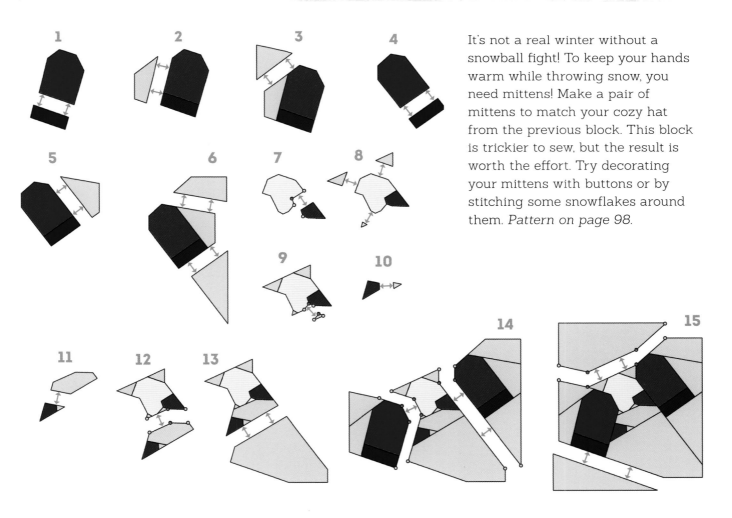

It's not a real winter without a snowball fight! To keep your hands warm while throwing snow, you need mittens! Make a pair of mittens to match your cozy hat from the previous block. This block is trickier to sew, but the result is worth the effort. Try decorating your mittens with buttons or by stitching some snowflakes around them. *Pattern on page 98.*

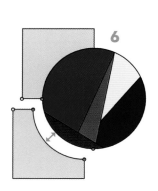

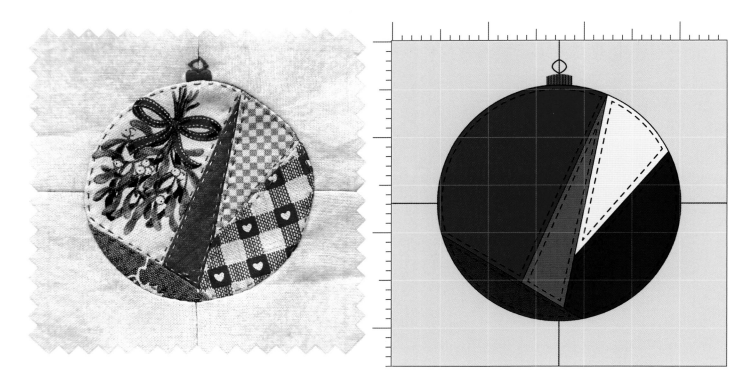

Ball Ornament

For me, Christmas is a cozy time at home—and time to decorate the Christmas tree! Here is the first of five ornament blocks that I made during my 365-day challenge, and it features a ball ornament. This block is very simple to make. I decorated it with backstitching in two different thread colors, but you can use whatever stitches and colors you'd like. *Pattern on page 98.*

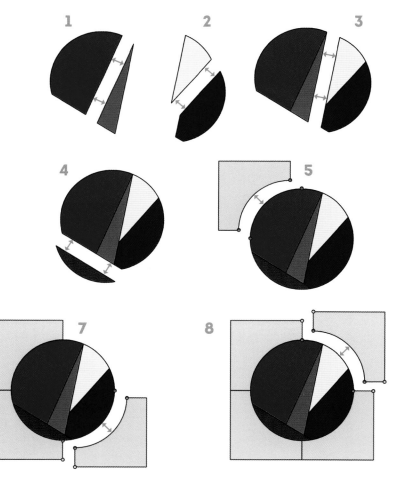

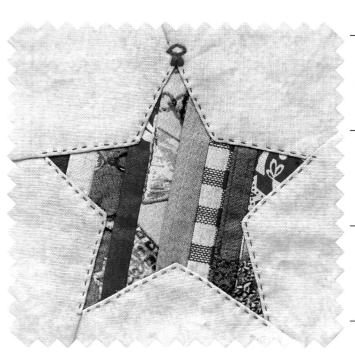

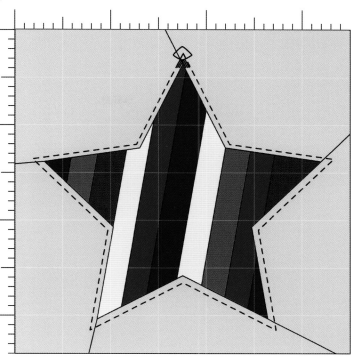

Star Ornament

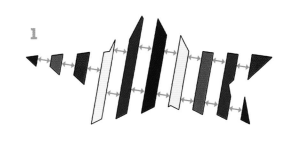

This magical star is my next Christmas ornament block. For this block, I decided to use mini fabric strips of the same width instead of randomly shaped fabric pieces. It is easy to decorate with whatever stitches you'd like; I backstitched around the star with red thread. *Pattern on page 98.*

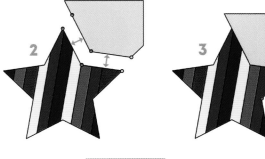

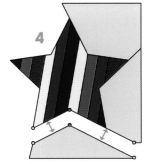

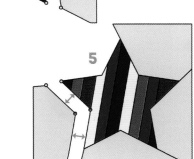

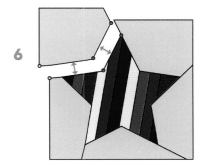

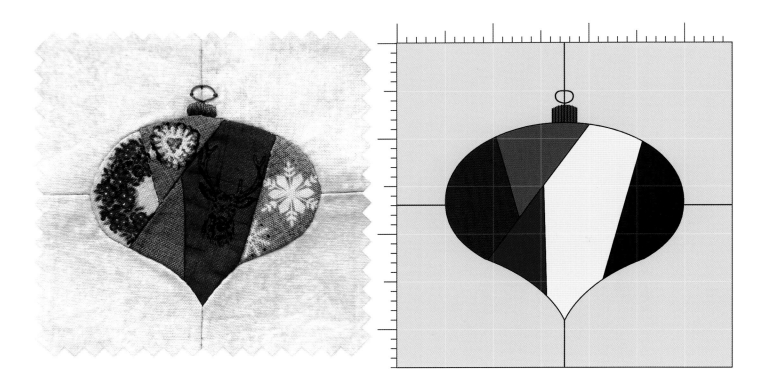

Icicle Ornament

My third ornament block, the icicle, is very tricky to sew because of its shape. For variation, try fabric scraps in crazy shapes and decorate with different stitches. *Pattern on page 99.*

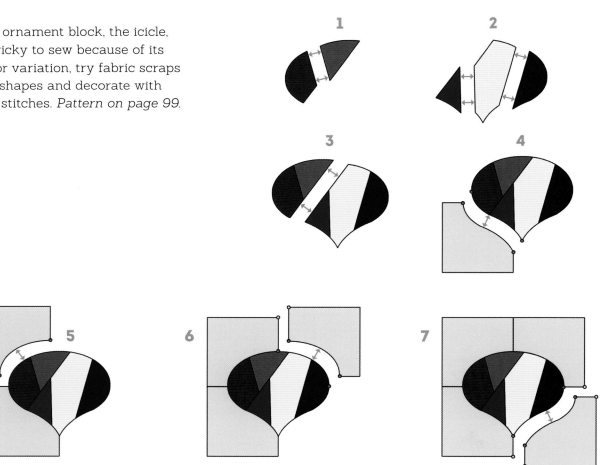

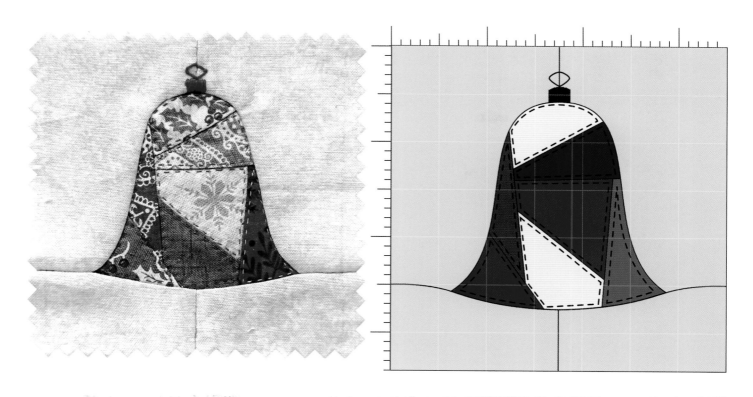

Bell Ornament

This jingly bell is the fourth Christmas ornament in my challenge. The block is quick to sew in your preferred stitch. I backstitched with three colors of thread. *Pattern on page 99.*

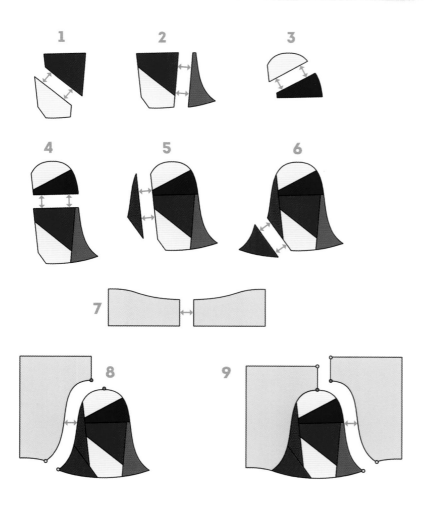

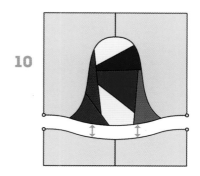

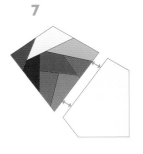
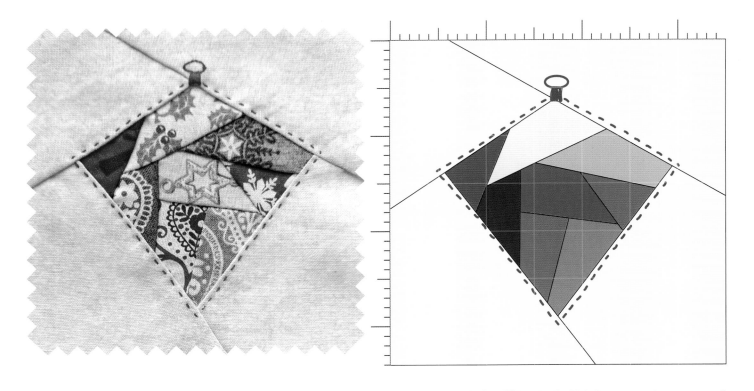

Diamond Ornament

My mother had a special box that held her childhood Christmas ornaments, and I remember a very unique diamond-shaped one. When I was young, I loved to lie on the floor and watch how this ornament reflected the Christmas lights. This block is very easy to sew and would be an amazing design for a table runner or fabric drink coasters. The diamond ornament is the fifth and last Christmas ornament in my challenge. *Pattern on page 99.*

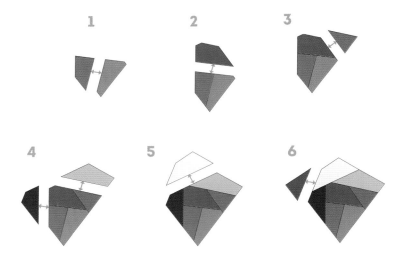

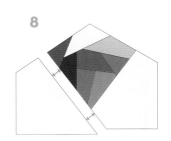
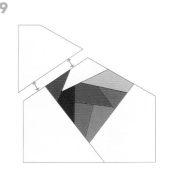
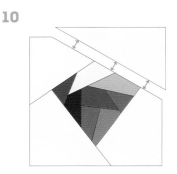

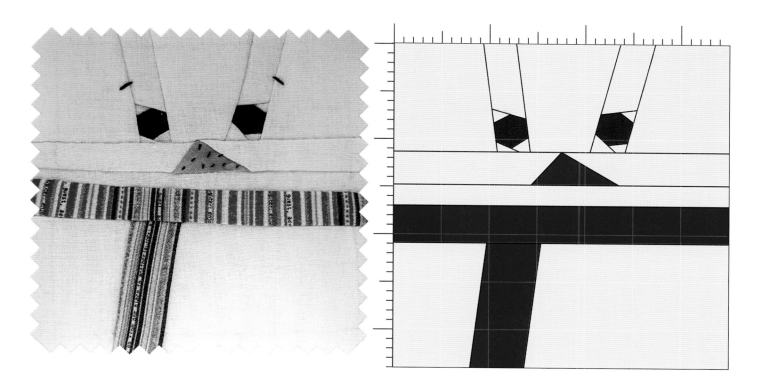

Close-Up Snowman

My inspiration for Day 221 of the *#365daysquiltscraps* challenge was my young daughter showing me some of her artwork with a magnifying glass. Here's a snowman from one of her drawings as he looked back at me through the glass. *Pattern on page 99.*

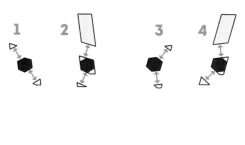

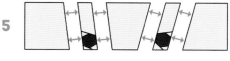

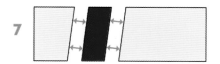

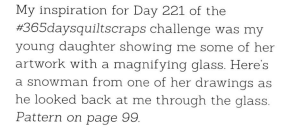

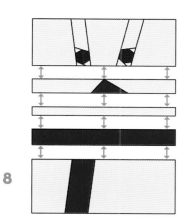

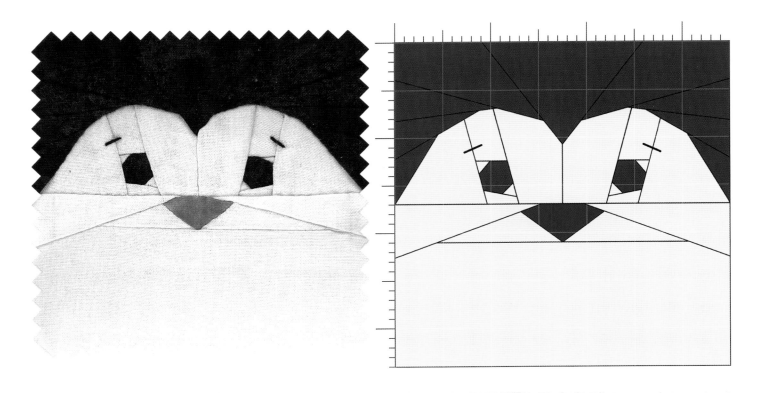

Close-Up Penguin

This curious little penguin, also seen through a magnifying glass, is a good friend of the snowman from my previous block. The details of how this block is constructed are very interesting. *Pattern on page 100.*

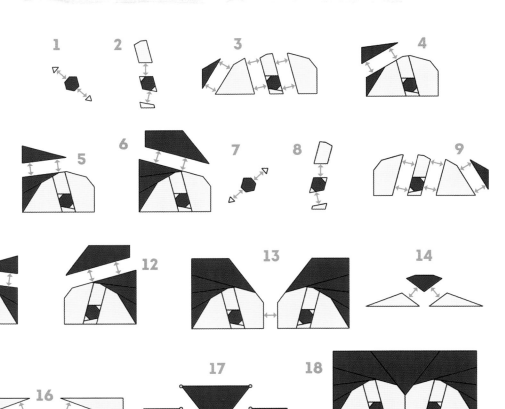

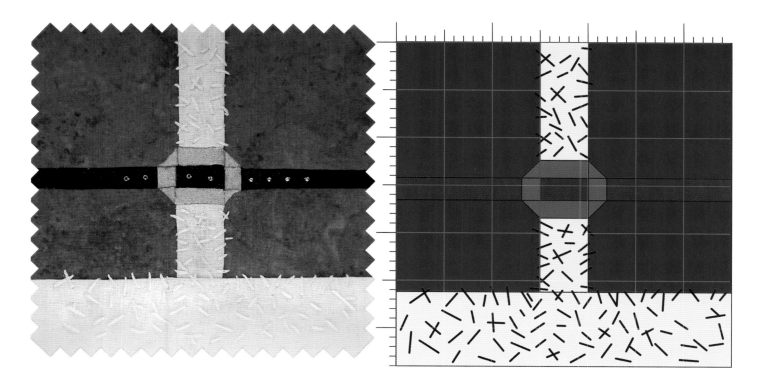

Santa's Belt

When I started Santa's belt, I wanted to make a white buckle, but then I remembered that I had some golden fabric dye, so I painted it and then used tiny beads as the holes. Some crazy white stitches created the furry edging on Santa's coat. If you do not have fabric dye, you can use fabric with metallic elements. *Pattern on page 100.*

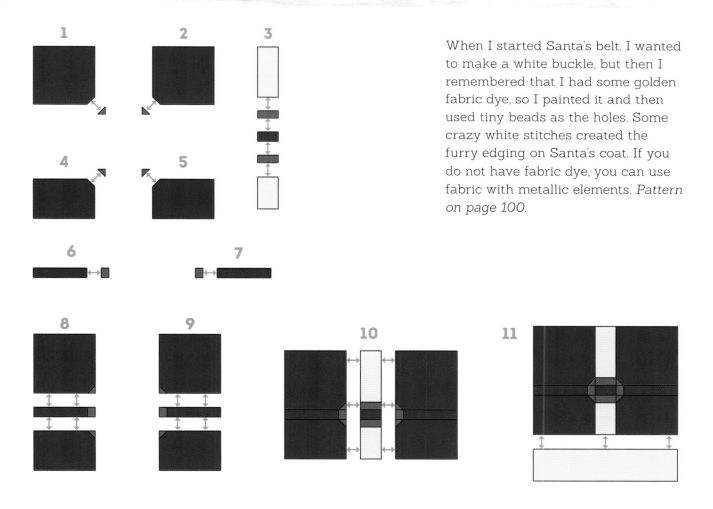

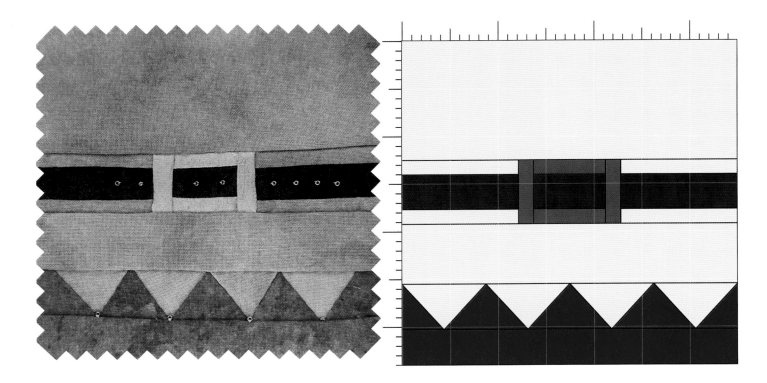

An Elf's Belt

This block is a belt worn by one of Santa's elves. I painted this belt buckle just as I did with Santa's in the previous block, and then I used tiny beads as the holes and as bells on the trim of the jacket. Instead of beads, you could decorate with buttons, stitches, or French knots. *Pattern on page 100.*

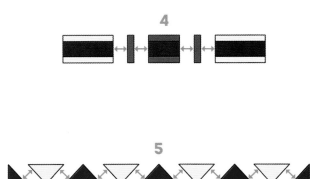

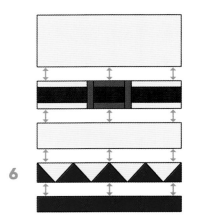

PART TWO

Spooky Halloween

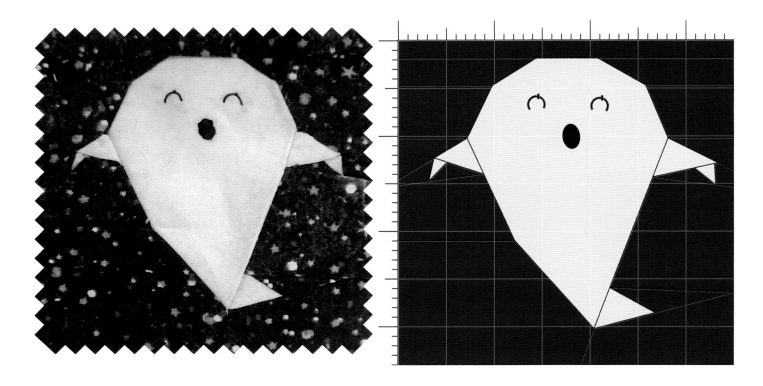

Friendly Ghost

Many people think of ghosts as being scary, but I don't think they are out to harm us. Instead, I think ghosts are very curious and just want to talk! Some of them may look frightening, which can be an obstacle when trying to make friends, but my ghost is very friendly looking, so don't be afraid! *Pattern on page 100.*

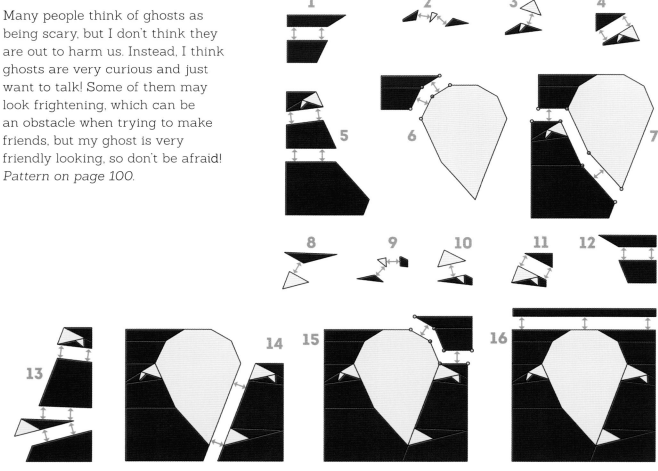

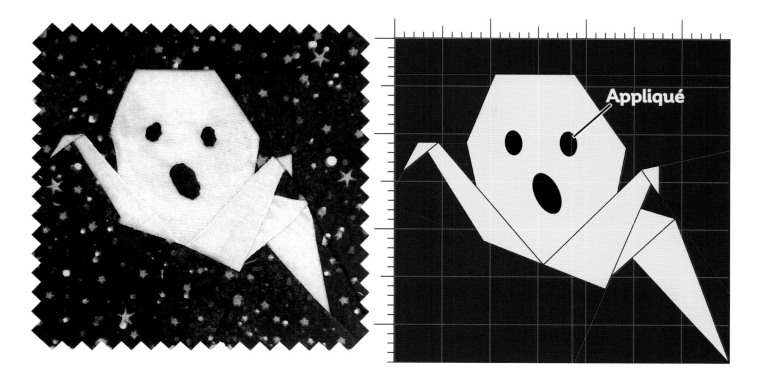

Appliqué

Screaming Ghost

"Wait for me! I don't want to miss the Halloween fun!" This ghost is the life of the party and is constructed with a combination of piecing and blind-stitching appliqué. It was a lot of fun to hand-appliqué the small pieces for the eyes and mouth. *Pattern on page 101.*

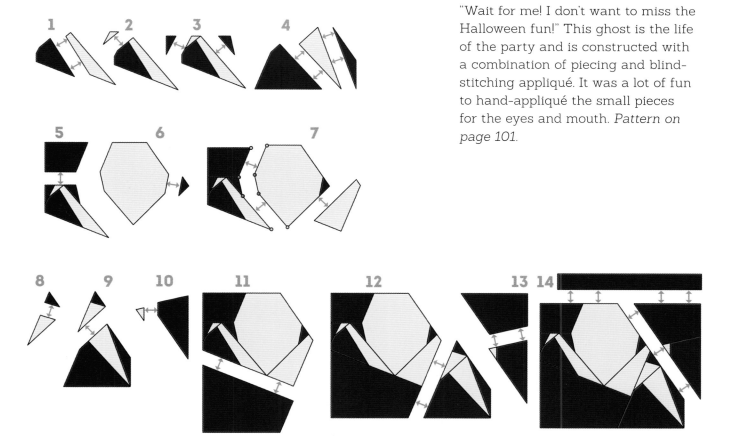

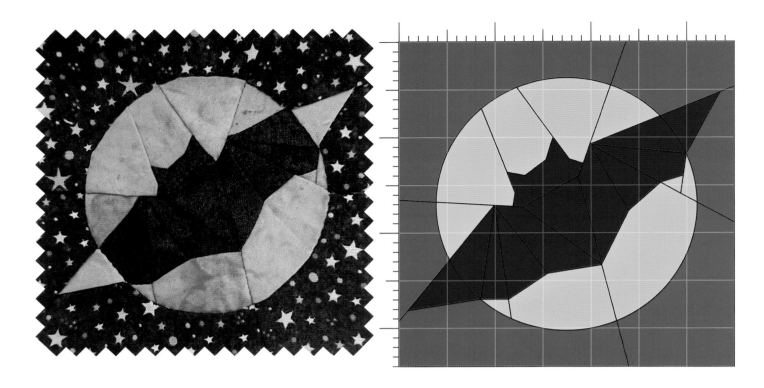

Almost Dracula

As you all know, vampires have the power to transform into bats. As I made this design, I was thinking about Dracula from the *Hotel Transylvania* movies. This block shows the shadow of the bat against the moon. It was tricky to sew every piece of the moon, but I was very happy with the result! *Pattern on page 101.*

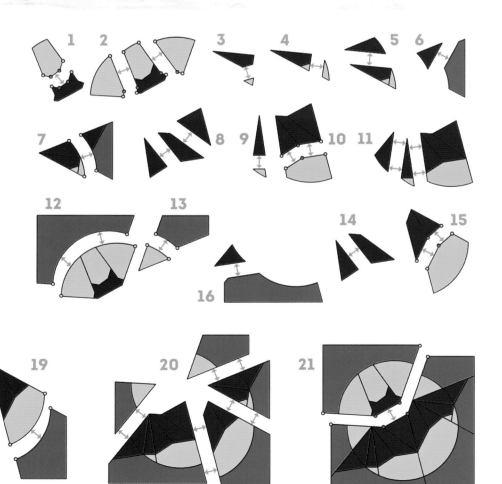

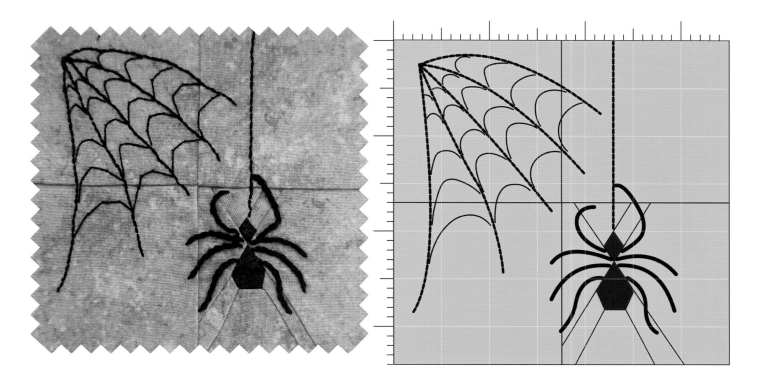

Spider

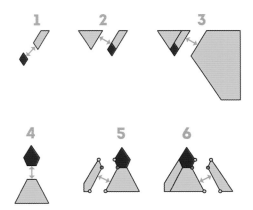

Unlike me, my husband is a *big fan* of spiders! So I just had to make a Halloween block featuring a spider. In this block, I used two different embroidery hand stitches: backstitching and outline stitching. *Pattern on page 101.*

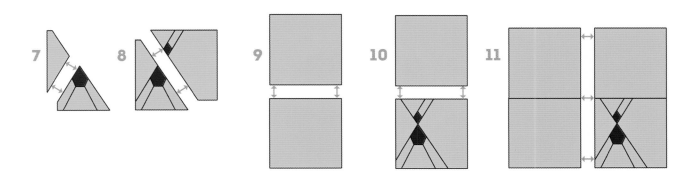

Witch on a Broom

One of the most popular Halloween characters is the witch. I love witches, but I don't like when they're drawn with green faces. This block is very quick to sew. I used two different embroidery hand stitches: backstitching and outline stitching. *Pattern on page 101.*

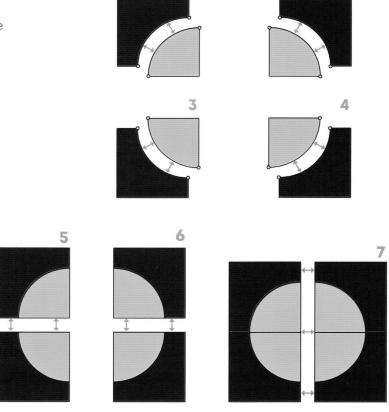

Redheaded Good Witch

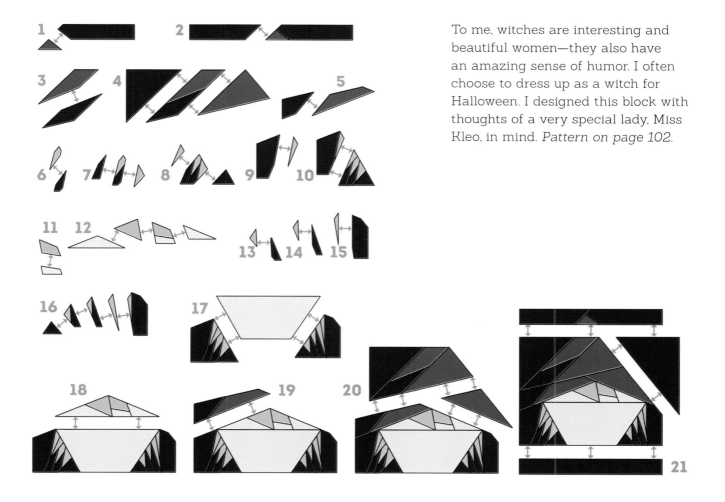

To me, witches are interesting and beautiful women—they also have an amazing sense of humor. I often choose to dress up as a witch for Halloween. I designed this block with thoughts of a very special lady, Miss Kleo, in mind. *Pattern on page 102.*

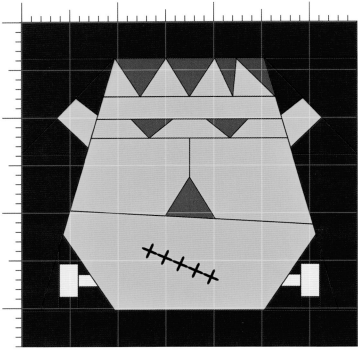

Frankenstein

Frankenstein's monster is a fictional character who first appeared in Mary Shelley's novel *Frankenstein, or The Modern Prometheus*. In the book, the author describes the monster as 8 feet tall and hideously ugly but sensitive and emotional, so I made my version with a smile and kind eyes. This block was finished for Day 128 of my *#365daysquiltscraps* challenge. *Pattern on page 102.*

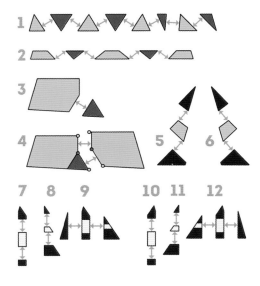

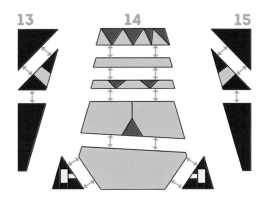

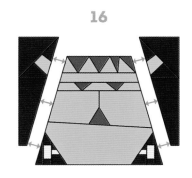

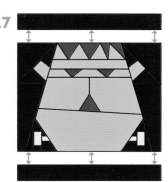

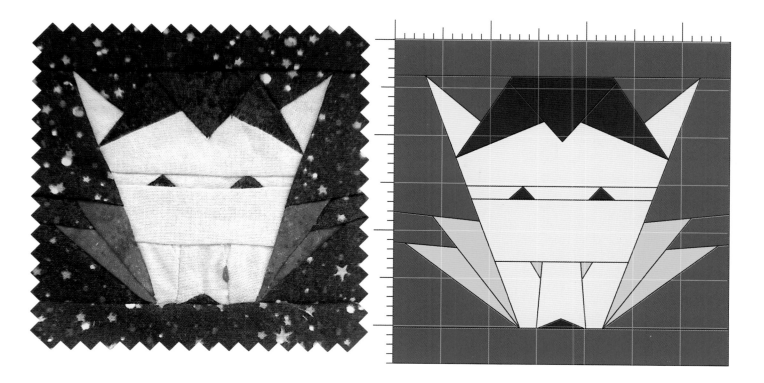

Dracula

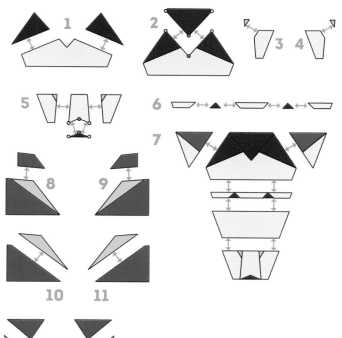

Dracula is a scary character, but he's the coolest guy in Transylvania. I decided to stitch a red drop falling from one of his teeth, but don't worry—it's just tomato juice! Be very careful when sewing the tiny pieces, such as the teeth. *Pattern on page 102.*

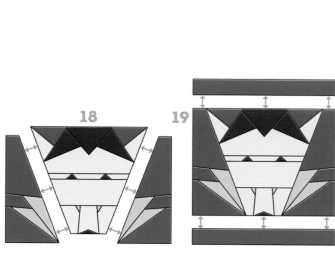

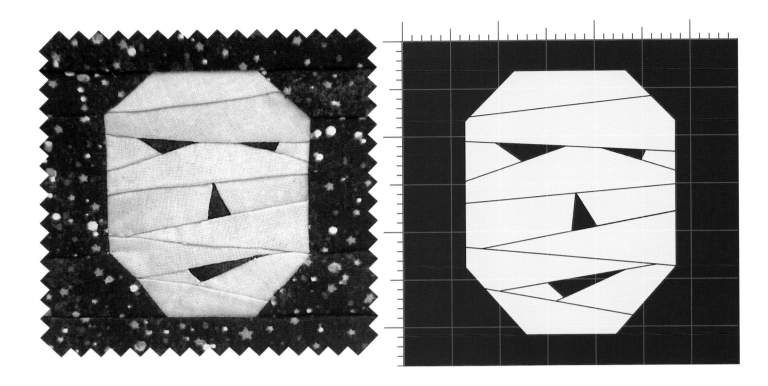

Mummy

I designed this mummy for Day 138 of my challenge. He reminds me of a mummy that was running around and chasing everyone in a classic *DuckTales* cartoon from the late 1980s. Because the main pieces are all the same color and some are similar shapes, be careful that you sew them together in the right order! *Pattern on page 102.*

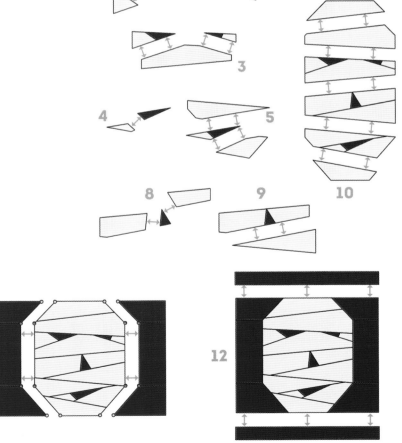

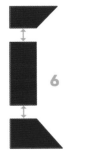

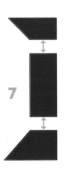

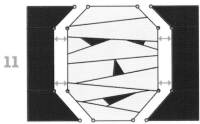

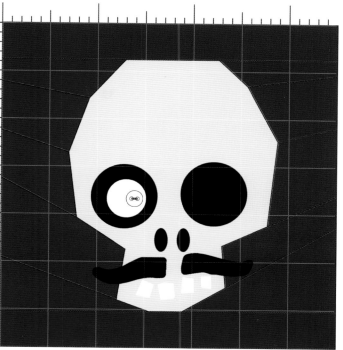

Skull with a Mustache

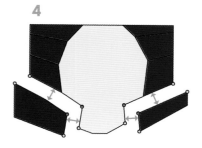

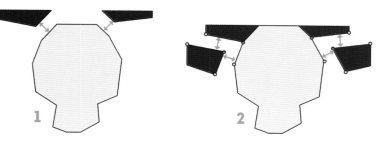

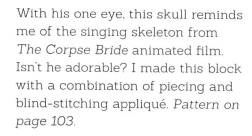

With his one eye, this skull reminds me of the singing skeleton from *The Corpse Bride* animated film. Isn't he adorable? I made this block with a combination of piecing and blind-stitching appliqué. *Pattern on page 103*.

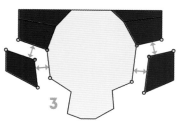

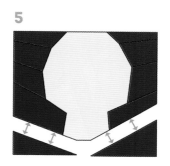

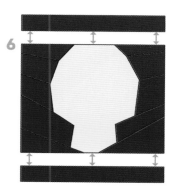

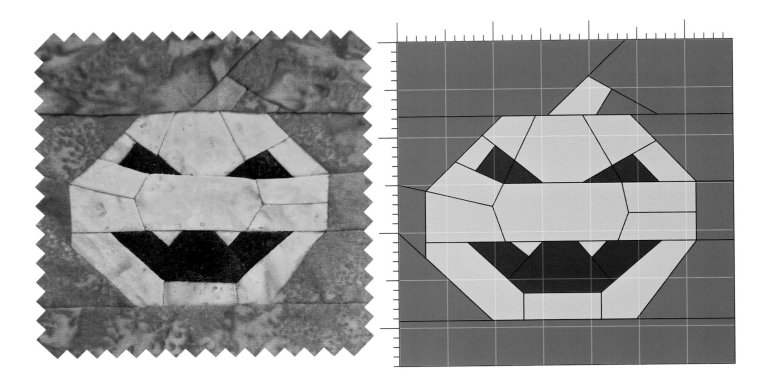

Spooky Pumpkin

Let me introduce you to my new Halloween friend, the menacing-looking Mr. Pumpkin. Is he scary enough? The hardest parts of this block to sew are the teeth. Another option for this block is to choose green fabric for the body and yellow fabric for the eyes and mouth to make it look as if there is a candle inside. *Pattern on page 103.*

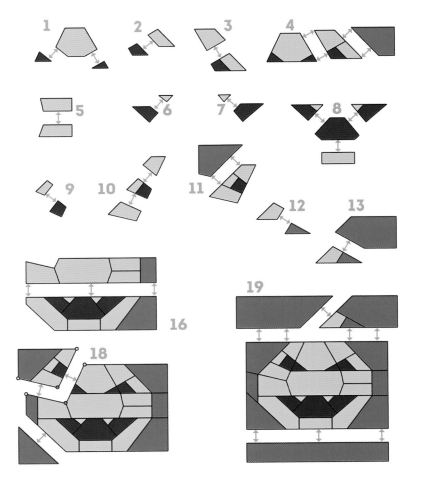

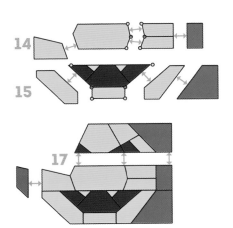

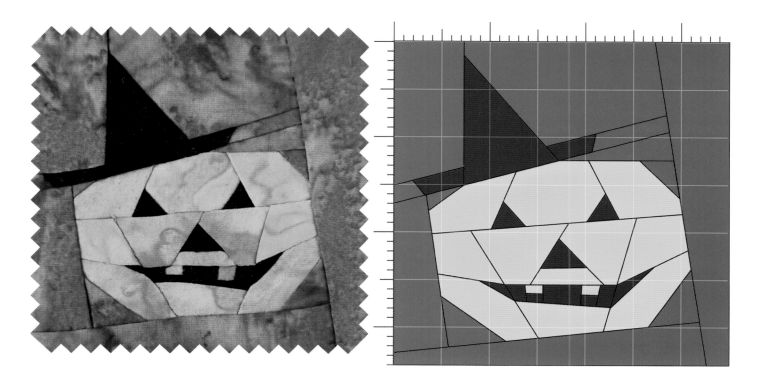

Pumpkin in a Witch's Hat

Is this pumpkin full of spooky thoughts or happiness? Is he ready to scare or care? In this block, the hat and teeth can both be tricky to sew, so be careful with these pieces. As with the previous block, you can make this pumpkin's body green, with yellow eyes and nose, to give the impression of a candle inside. *Pattern on page 103.*

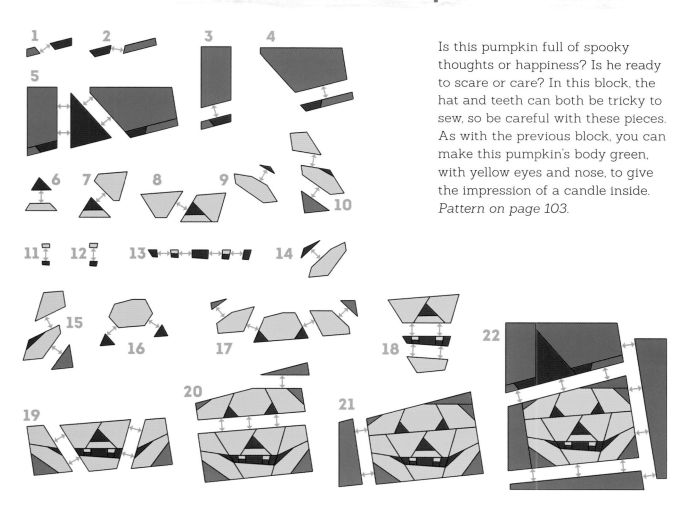

Smiling Pumpkin

There's no doubt that this pumpkin is happy to meet you! I sewed all of this block's details with blind-stitching appliqué by hand. *Pattern on page 103.*

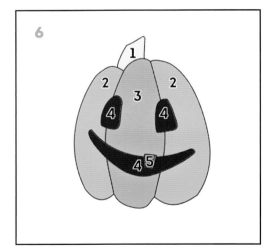

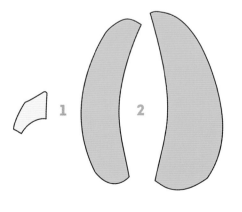

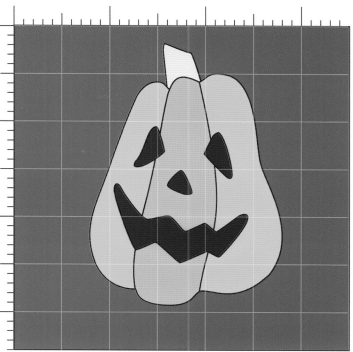

Scary Pumpkin

This pumpkin is trying to be scary, but isn't he adorable? I made this Halloween block for Day 150 of my *#365daysquiltscraps* challenge, using blind-stitching appliqué for the entire project. *Pattern on page 104.*

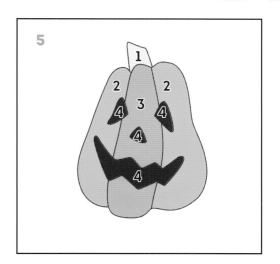

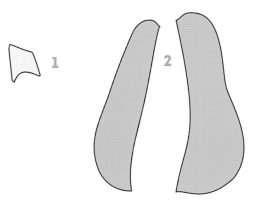

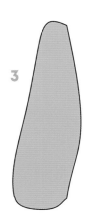

PART THREE

Easter Joy

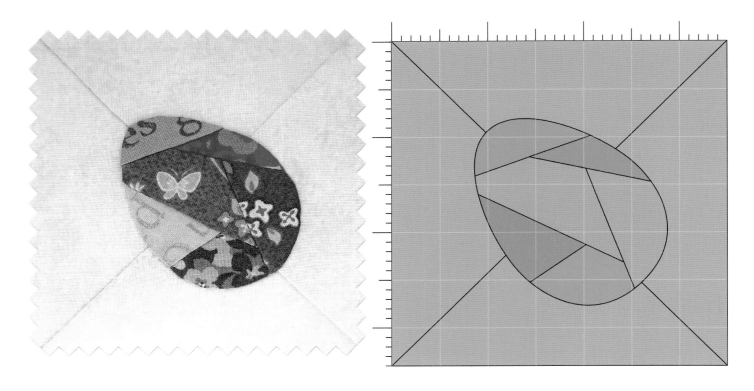

Modern Egg

There are so many types of Easter decorations, and Easter eggs are among the most popular. I decided to put a modern spin on the traditional Easter egg with bold colors and abstract shapes. *Pattern on page 104.*

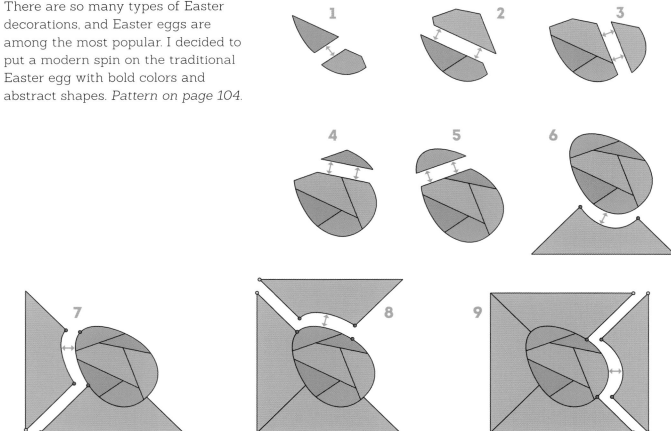

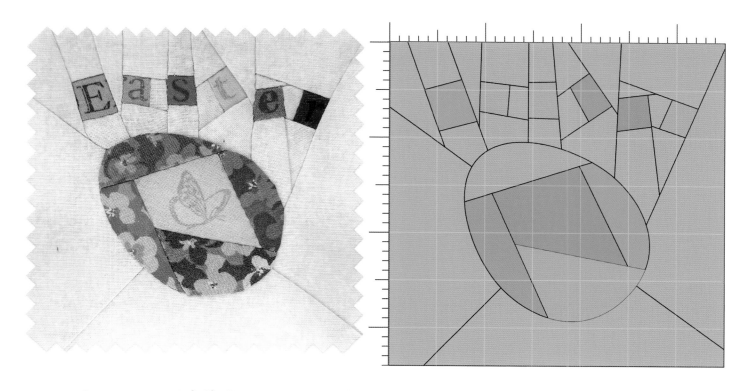

Egg Hunt

For this Easter egg design, I used letters that I cut out from different fabrics. You can stitch letters onto the block, as I did, or you can draw them. *Pattern on page 104.*

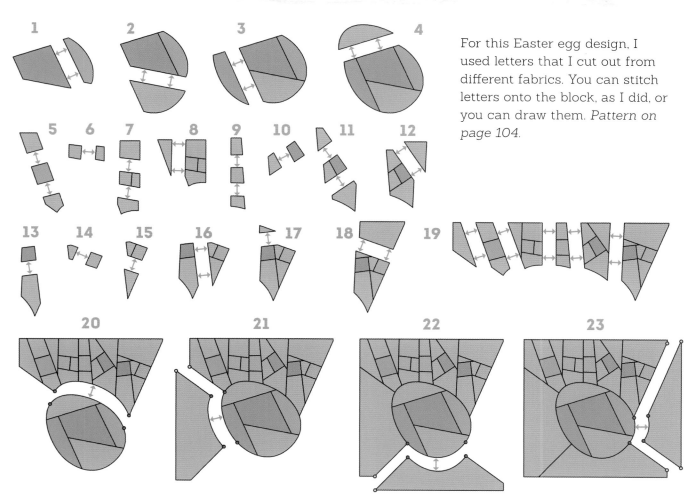

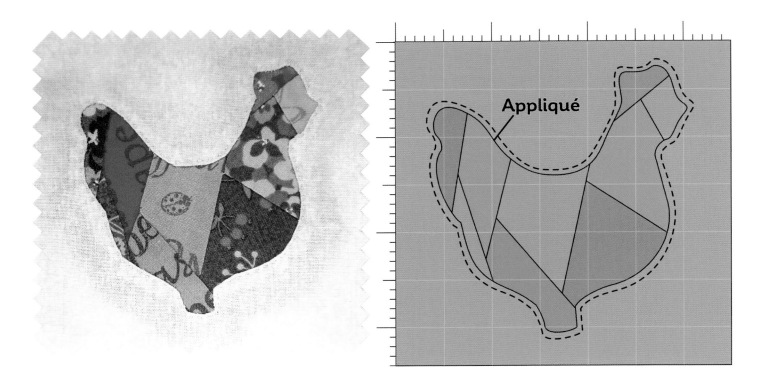

Colorful Hen

Easter is full of springtime spirit! For Day 346 of my 365-day challenge, I made this hen silhouette with a reverse appliqué technique. *Pattern on page 104.*

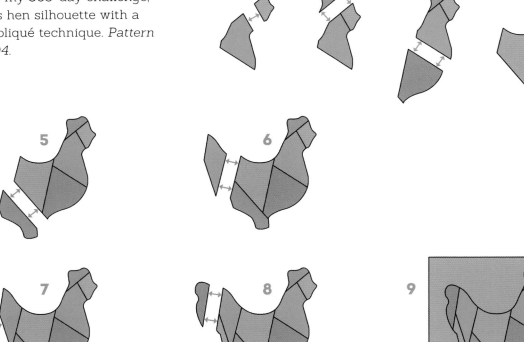

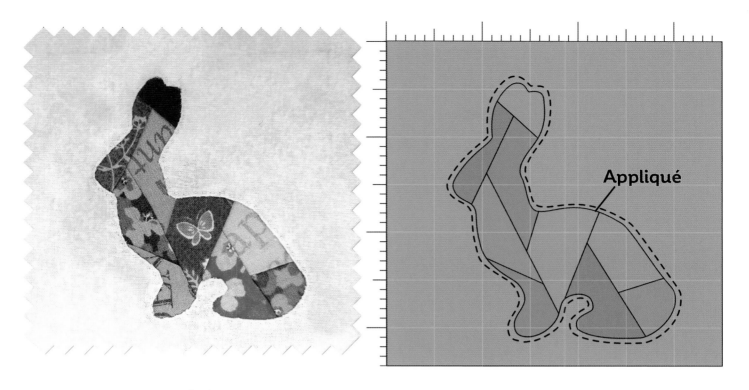

Appliqué

Rabbit Silhouette

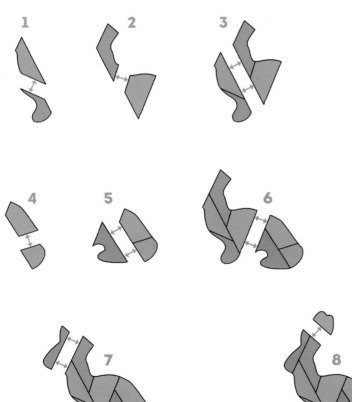

Here is my Easter bunny silhouette. I used reverse appliqué to sew this block, just like I did with the hen block. I love the finished look of this technique; it looks almost as if the silhouette was drawn by hand. For a bolder look, try decorating the silhouette with stitches. *Pattern on page 105.*

PART FOUR

Feline Friends

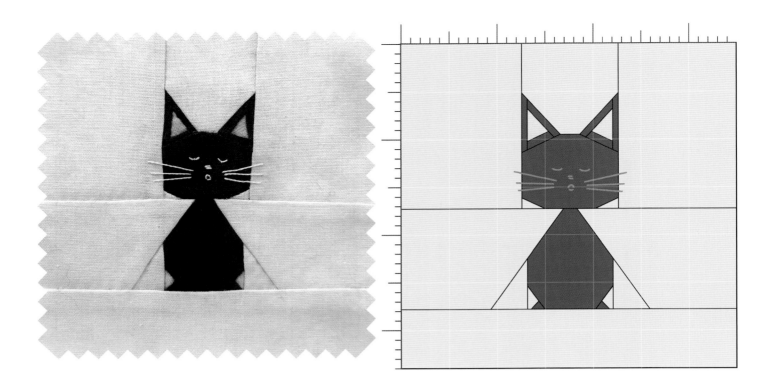

Otis the Gentleman

When we bought our first house, one of our neighbors had a black cat who they had adopted. Otis was quite the gentleman—I'd never before met a cat with such a special personality. In my native country, we have a tradition that before you enter your new house, you let a cat enter first to bring protection to the home. Otis was that cat for us! *Pattern on page 105*

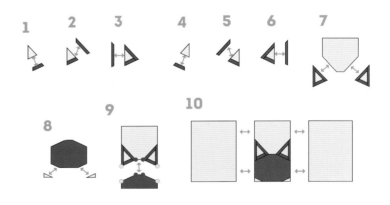

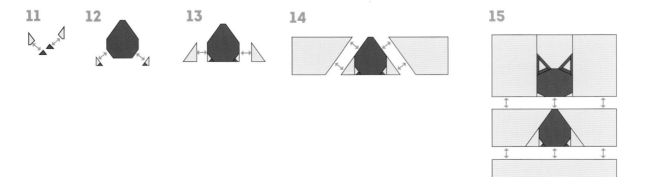

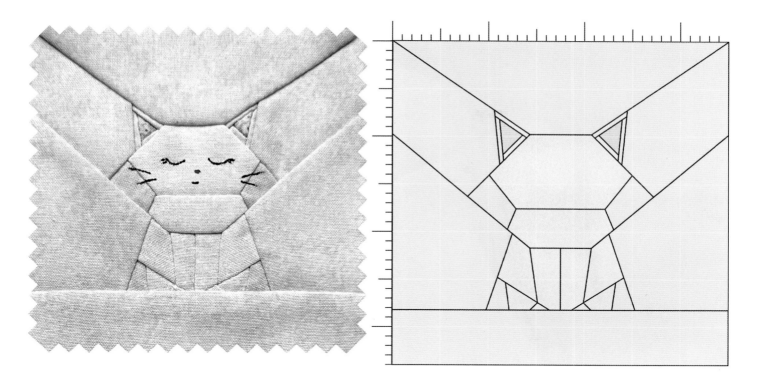

Friendly White Cat

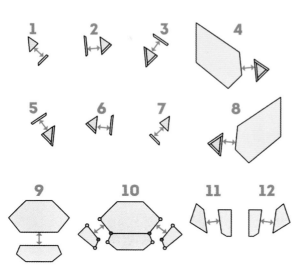

It's springtime, and love is in the air! Once, Otis disappeared, and we all helped look for him. He returned five days later, but he was not alone. He had found a girlfriend—a very sweet white cat (although she looked rather gray when we first saw her!). Our neighbors were so happy that Otis was home that they adopted his girlfriend and named her Lily. You can stitch or paint Lily's details. I used fabric paint for the eyes, lashes, nose, and whiskers. *Pattern on page 105.*

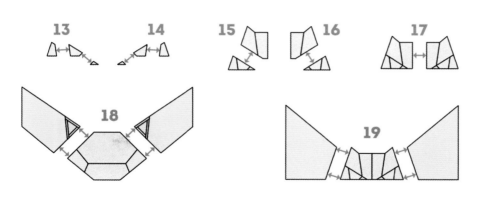

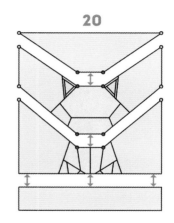

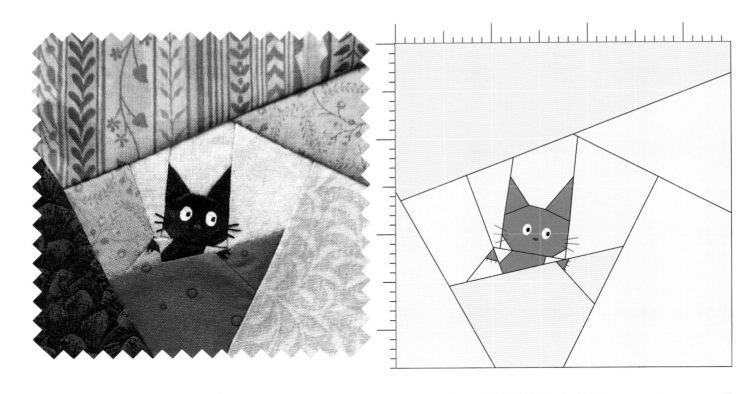

Curious Otis

We had a garden and a lot of trees in our yard, and Otis and Lily loved to sit on the fence and watch what was going on. Springtime was the best time, when the garden came alive with new smells, creatures, and adventures. Otis loved to jump for butterflies and flies, and he would always turn to look at Lily and make sure she was watching his brave attempts. In this block, I used a bold mix of colors around Otis's face, accented by both stitched and painted details. *Pattern on page 105.*

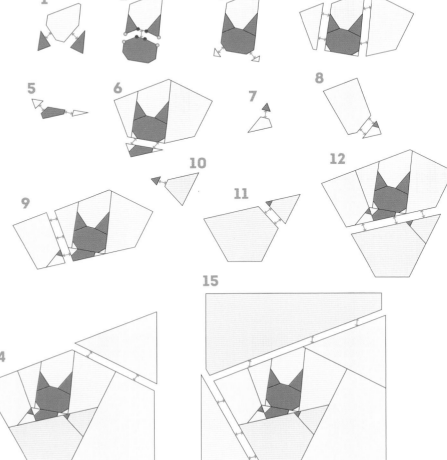

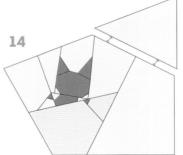

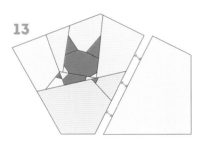

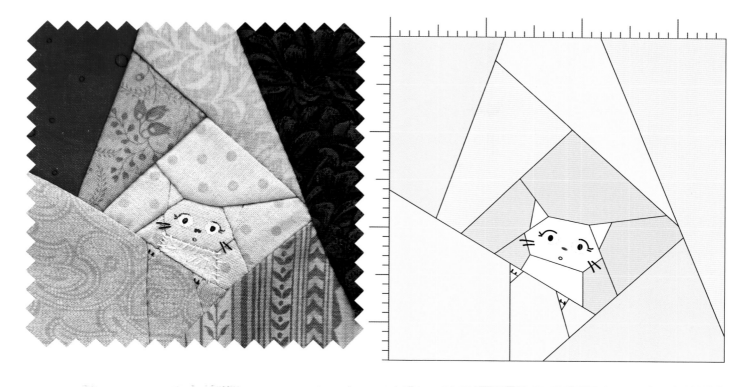

Peaceful Lily

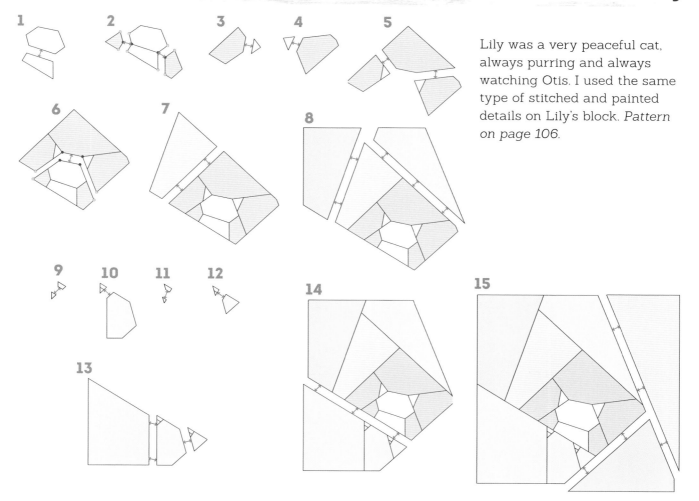

Lily was a very peaceful cat, always purring and always watching Otis. I used the same type of stitched and painted details on Lily's block. *Pattern on page 106.*

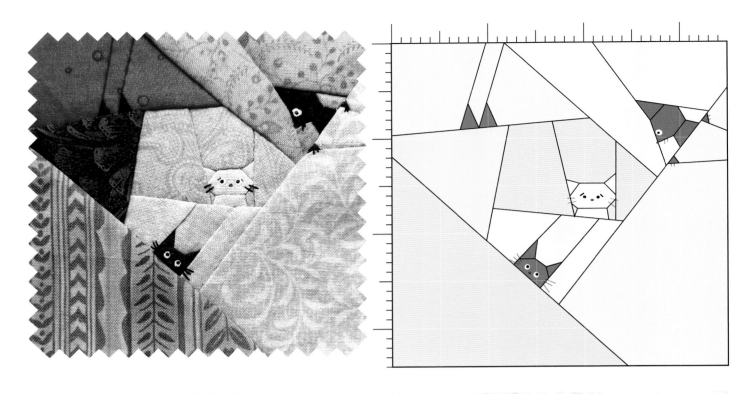

Little Kittens

It wasn't too long before Otis and Lily became parents to four adorable kittens who were full of life and curiosity. Our neighbors named the kittens Meowtie, Blackie, Pickle, and Soprano, and there are more stories about them in this book. *Pattern on page 106.*

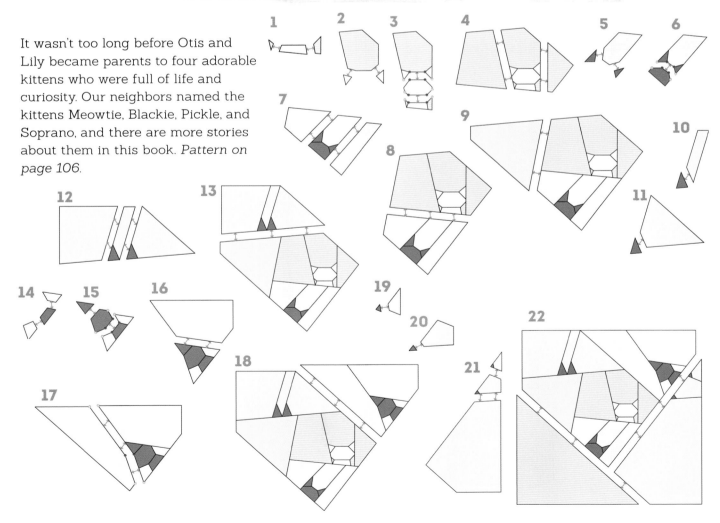

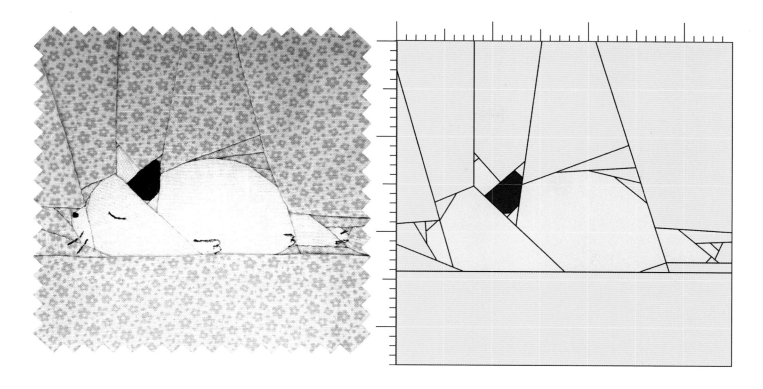

Soft Summer Nap

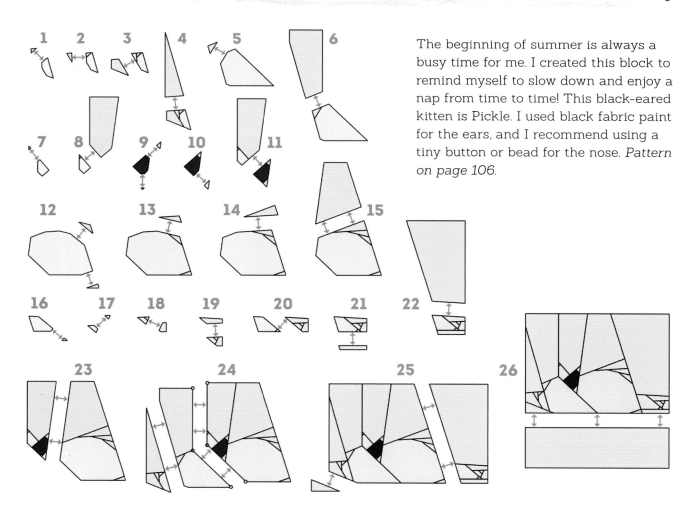

The beginning of summer is always a busy time for me. I created this block to remind myself to slow down and enjoy a nap from time to time! This black-eared kitten is Pickle. I used black fabric paint for the ears, and I recommend using a tiny button or bead for the nose. *Pattern on page 106.*

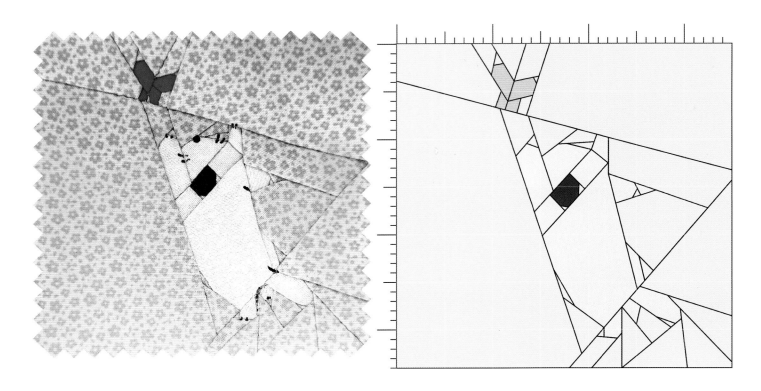

Butterfly Catcher

In this block, Pickle doesn't have time for a nap—it's a summer day, and it's time to chase butterflies! You can add to this block by stitching several more butterflies in different colors. *Pattern on page 106.*

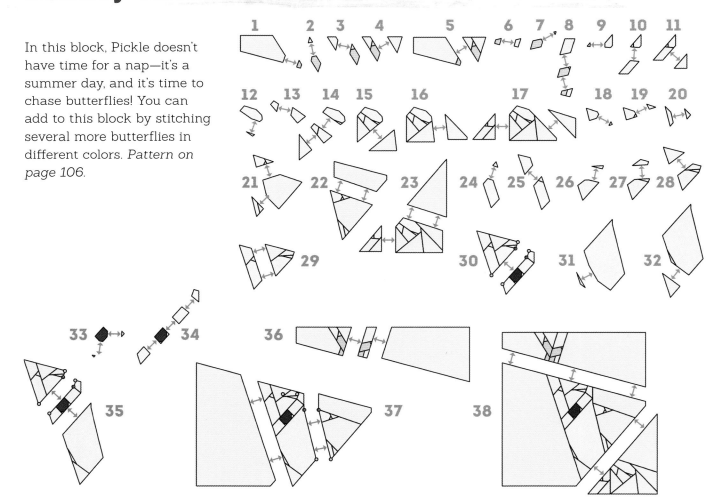

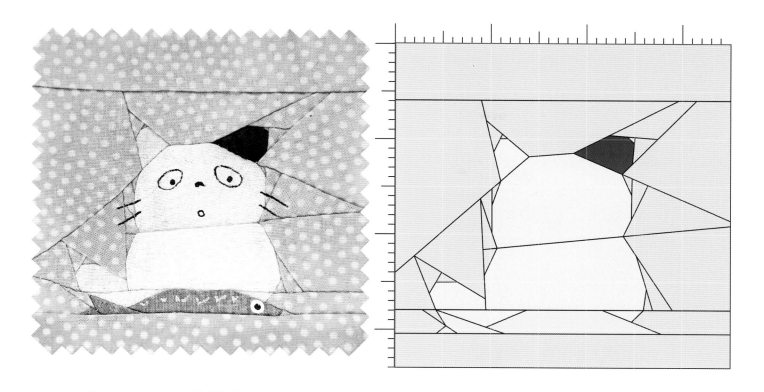

Lunchtime

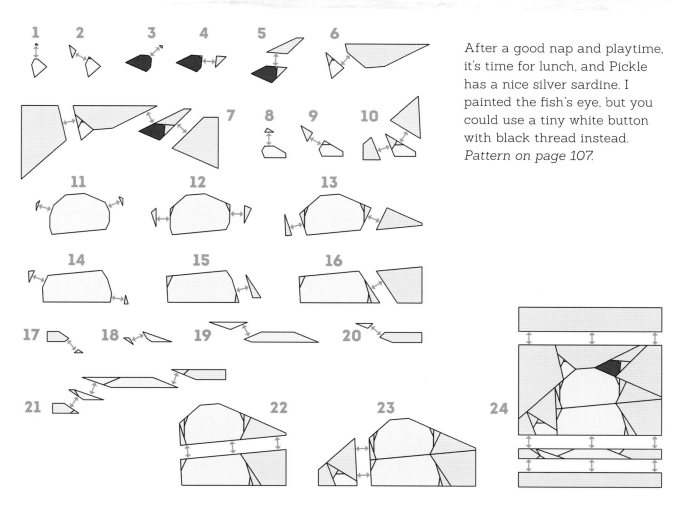

After a good nap and playtime, it's time for lunch, and Pickle has a nice silver sardine. I painted the fish's eye, but you could use a tiny white button with black thread instead. *Pattern on page 107.*

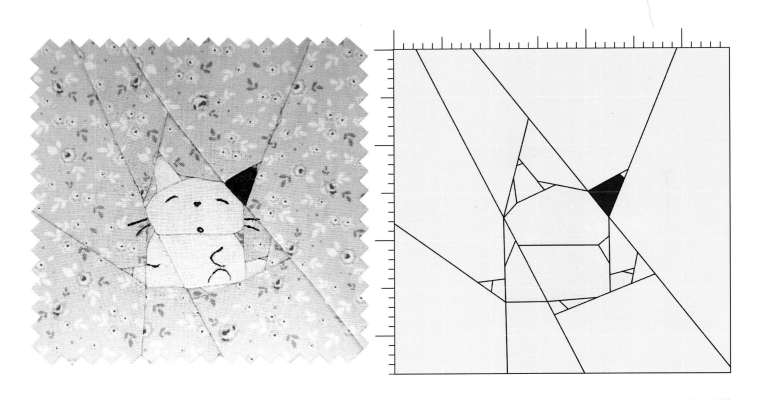

Siesta

Pickle the kitten is so soft and cute! After a busy summer day, he's ready for another nap. This block is incredibly easy to sew, and you can make it even easier by drawing in the details—then you'll have time for a nap, too! *Pattern on page 107.*

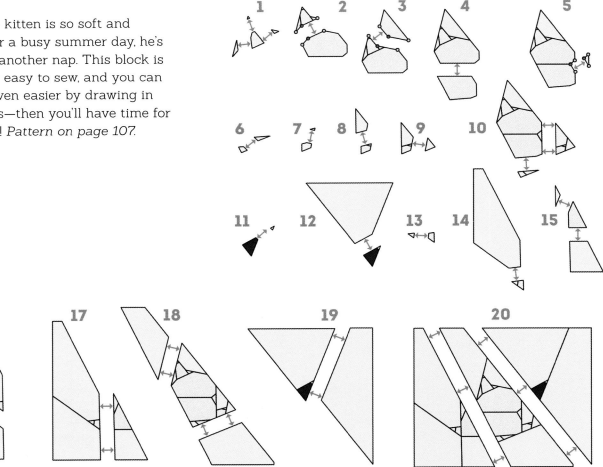

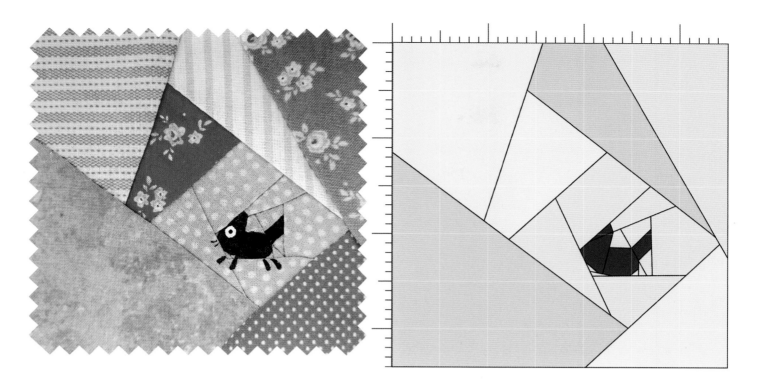

Cute Meowtie

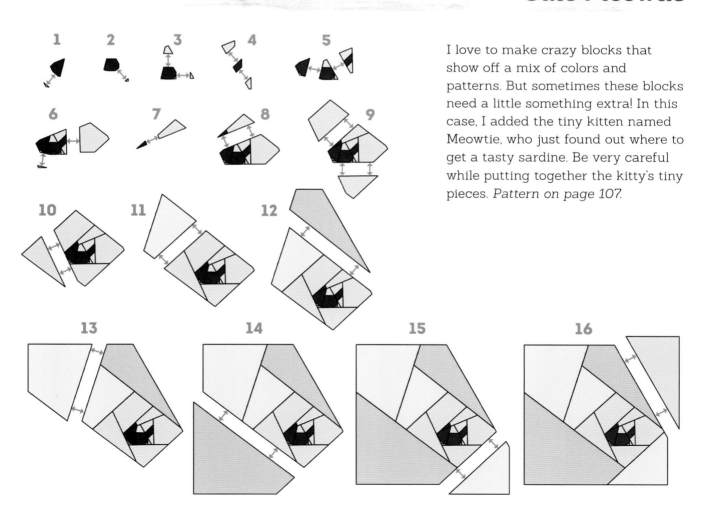

I love to make crazy blocks that show off a mix of colors and patterns. But sometimes these blocks need a little something extra! In this case, I added the tiny kitten named Meowtie, who just found out where to get a tasty sardine. Be very careful while putting together the kitty's tiny pieces. *Pattern on page 107.*

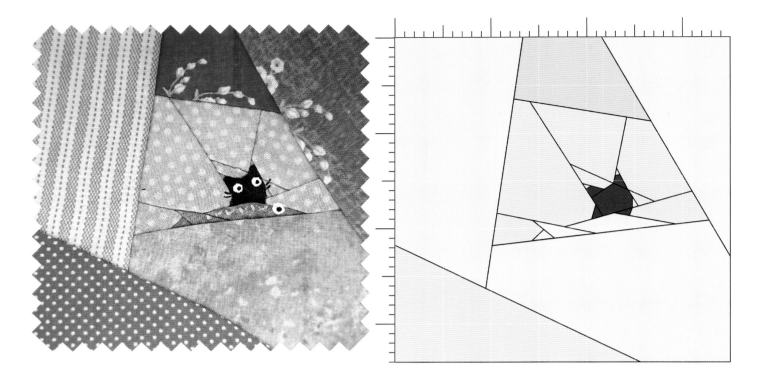

Meowtie's Prize

Tiny Meowtie got his prize: a big sardine for lunch! This is another block with a crazy combination of colors and designs. Experiment with different ways to add the details. *Pattern on page 107.*

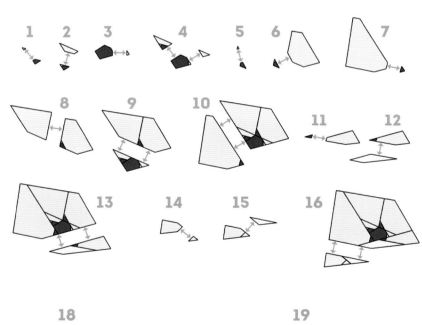

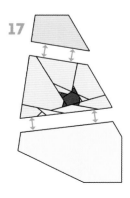
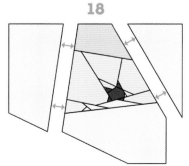
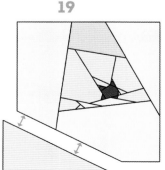

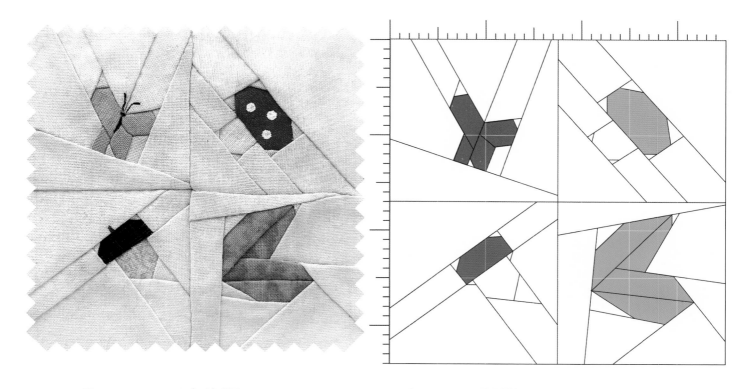

Forest Petites

This block is full of forest spirit: an acorn that will grow into a big, strong tree, a mushroom and some leaves to add splashes of color, and a charming butterfly. I used textile paint for the details, but stitched details would also look nice. Try different combinations, such as beads on the butterfly's head and French knots for the spots on the mushroom. *Pattern on page 108.*

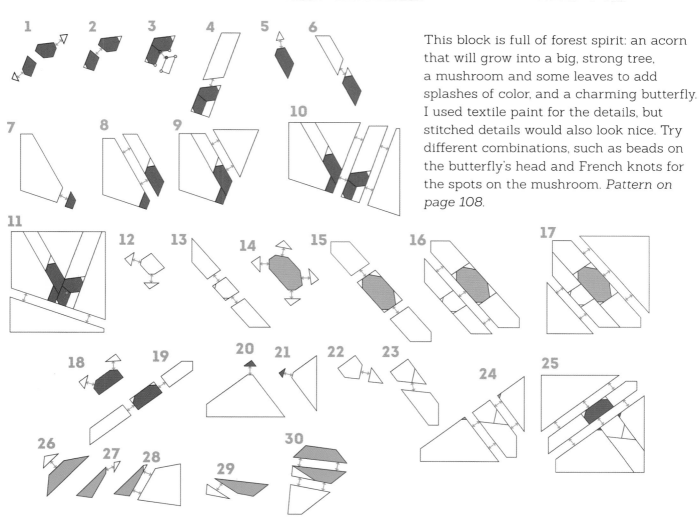

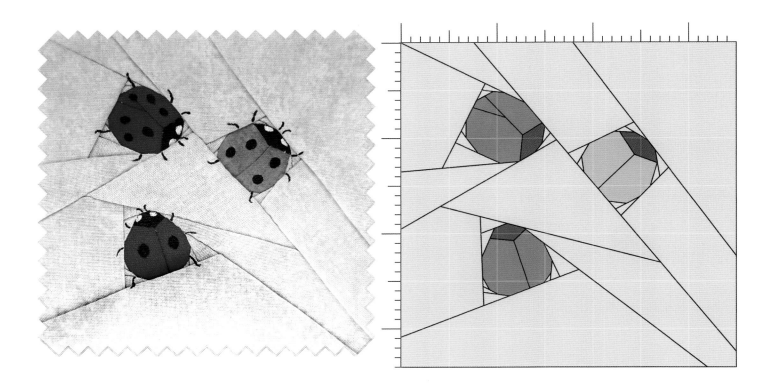

Forest Ladybugs

During one winter, my parents took care of a ladybug. They gave her a name and made special sugar water to feed her. This is a simple block to sew. I used paint for the details, but using beads, buttons, or stitches would give a 3-D effect. *Pattern on page 108.*

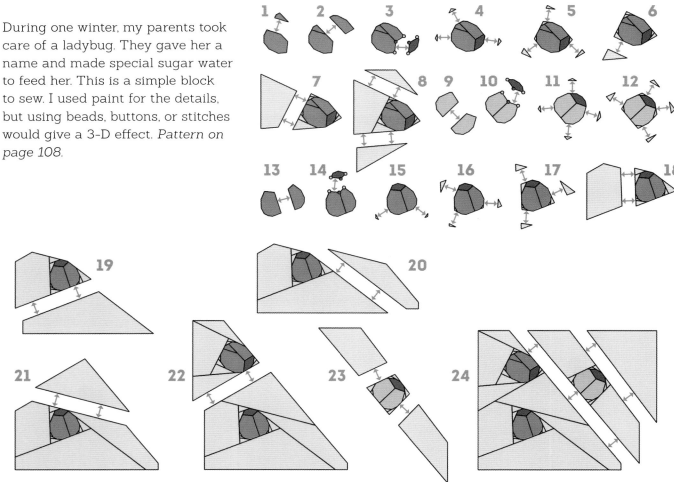

PART FIVE

Cat Yoga

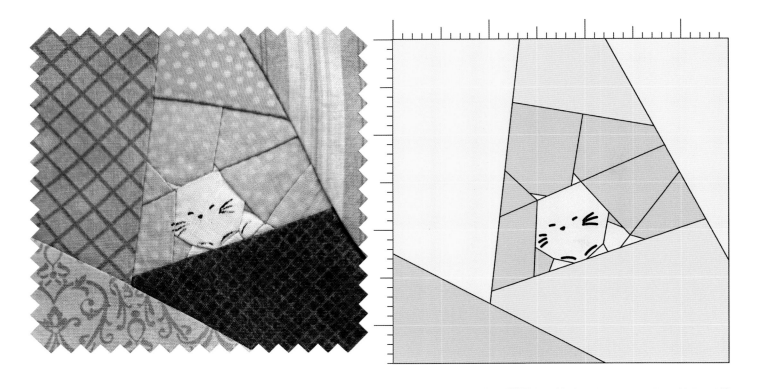

Time for Yoga

I designed cat yoga blocks during the last month of my #365daysquiltscraps challenge. Please meet Soprano, a white kitty who is a yoga expert! The tiny pieces, especially those that make up the cat, can be complicated to sew, so be careful. *Pattern on page 108.*

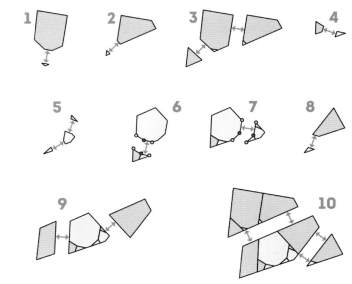

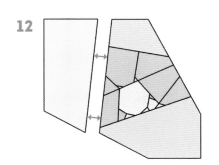

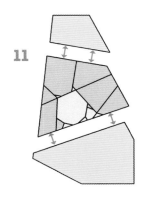

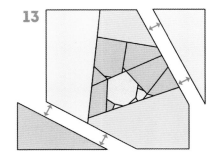

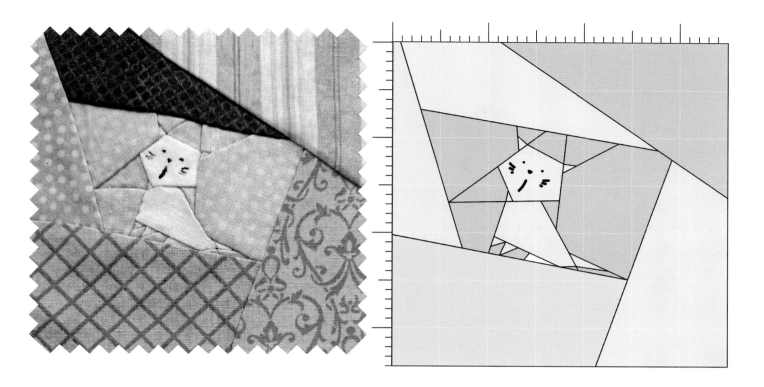

Soprano Is Awake

Soprano is awake and ready for cat yoga! You can stitch or draw/paint the details; I used black fabric paint. *Pattern on page 108.*

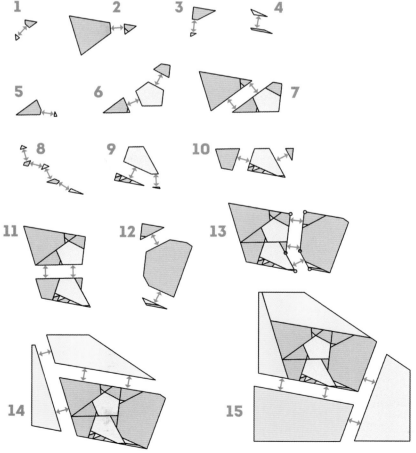

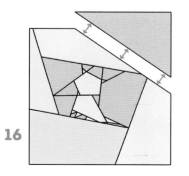

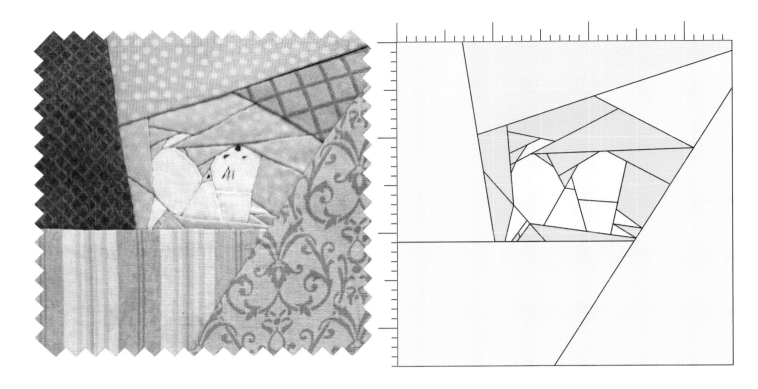

Cat Pose

Soprano starts her yoga with a cat pose. The background is relatively easy to sew, but the cat is made of many tiny pieces. Try different fabrics to give the block a bolder or softer color scheme. *Pattern on page 109.*

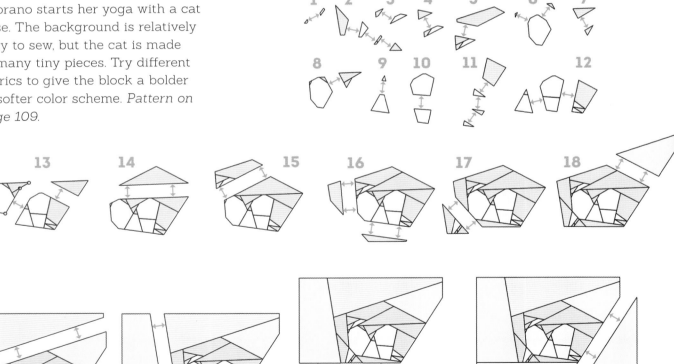

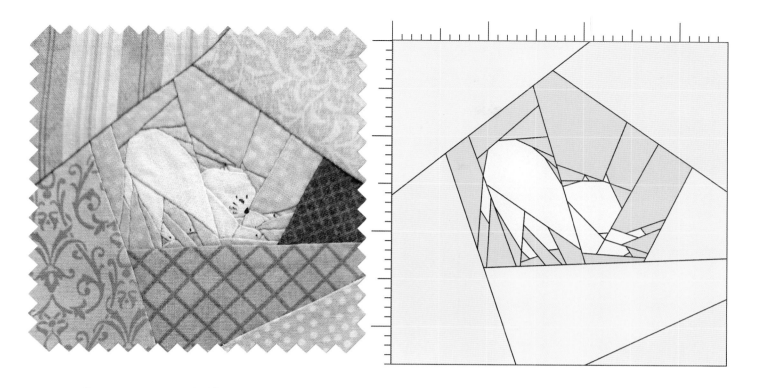

Puppy Pose

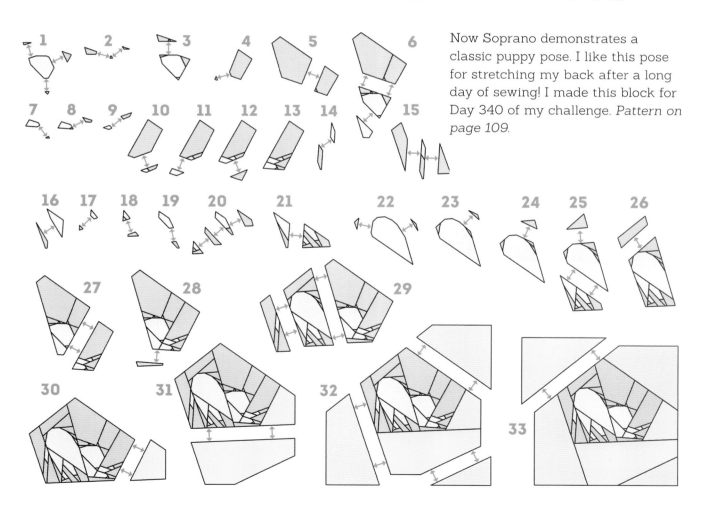

Now Soprano demonstrates a classic puppy pose. I like this pose for stretching my back after a long day of sewing! I made this block for Day 340 of my challenge. *Pattern on page 109.*

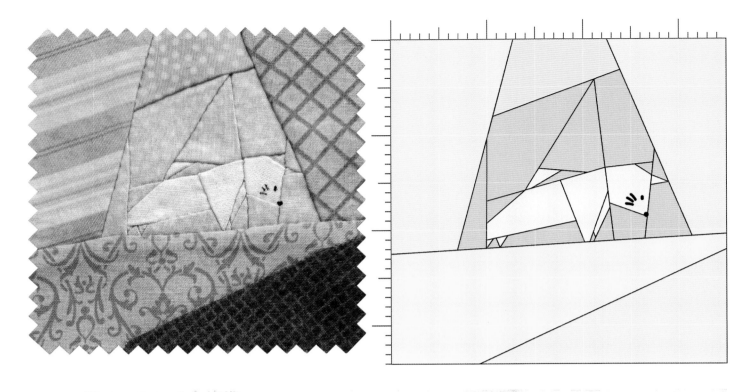

Planking Soprano

Soprano is in *phalakasana*, otherwise known as the plank pose. A French knot works well for the nose; if you choose to sew this block in a larger size, try a bead or button nose. *Pattern on page 109.*

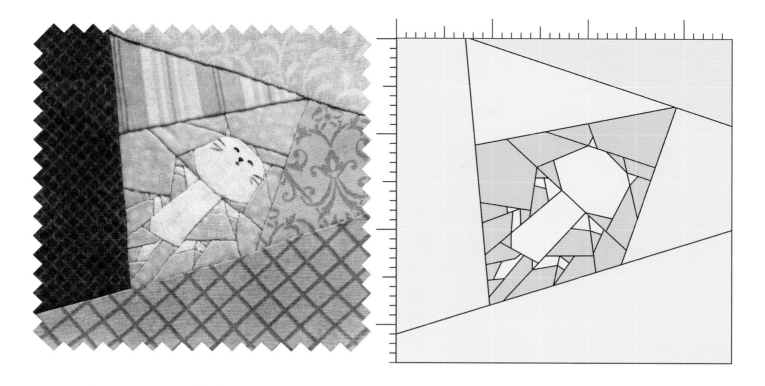

Resting in Corpse Pose

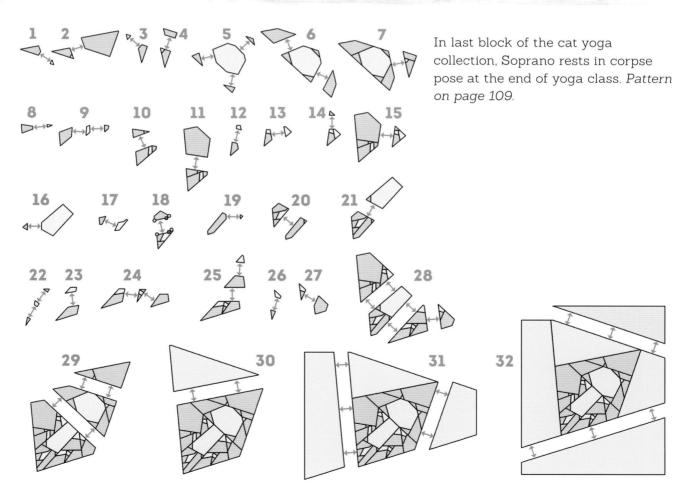

In last block of the cat yoga collection, Soprano rests in corpse pose at the end of yoga class. *Pattern on page 109.*

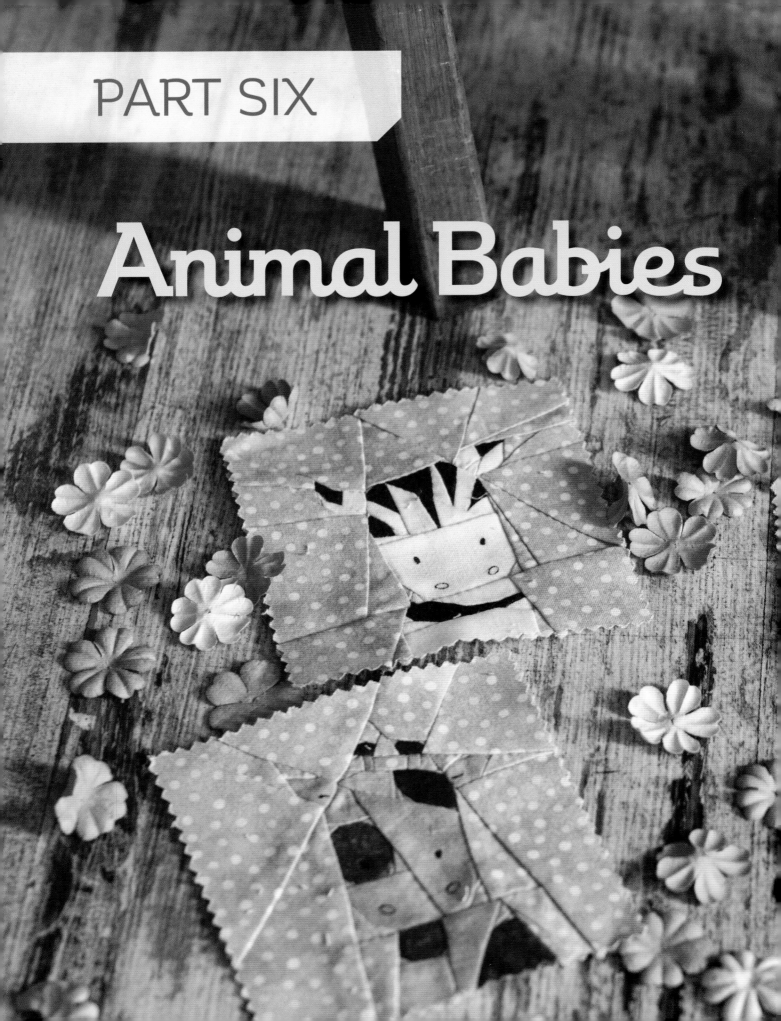

PART SIX

Animal Babies

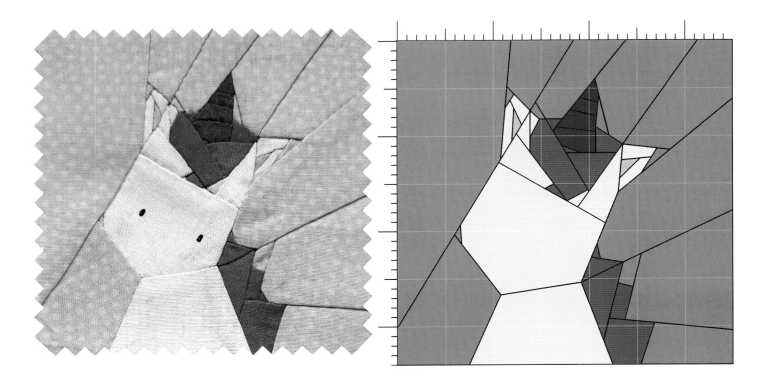

Baby Unicorn

I created this soft, cute unicorn as a special block for my daughter. I also love to incorporate it into quilts that I make for baby shower gifts. *Pattern on page 110.*

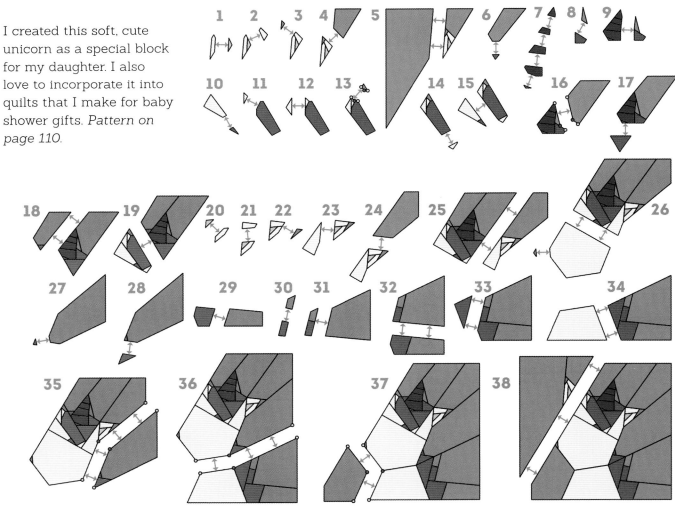

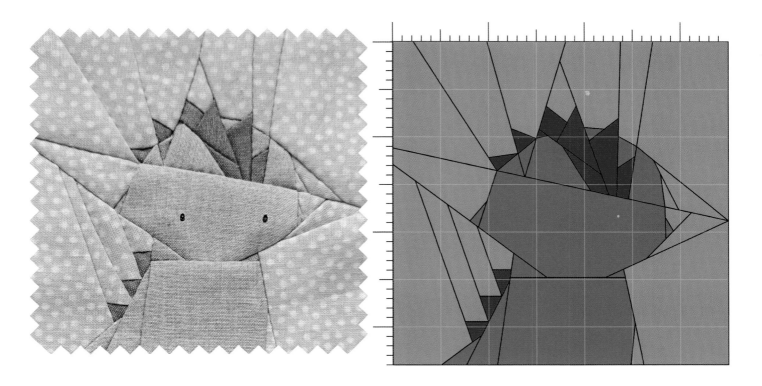

Baby Dragon

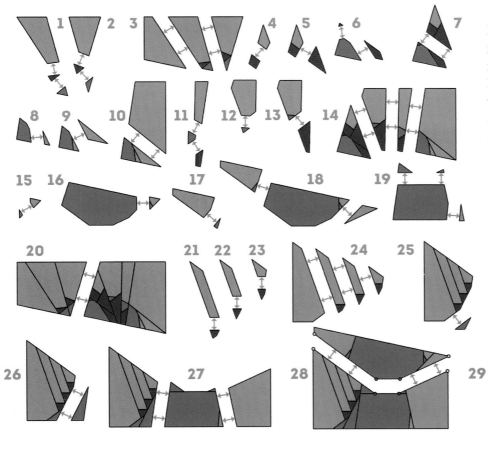

My daughter said, "Unicorn needs a friend. More magic, mommy!" So I created this little dragon. In my craft word, unicorns and dragons are best friends. On the face, I used fabric paint for the eyes and a water-based pigment ink pad for the rosy cheeks. *Pattern on page 110.*

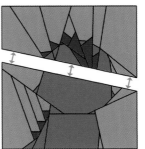

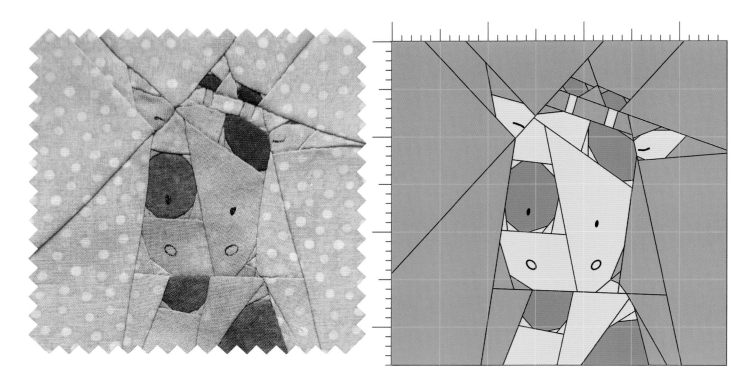

Giraffe Calf

This adorable little giraffe is another of my favorites for baby projects, such as blankets and nursery décor. *Pattern on page 110.*

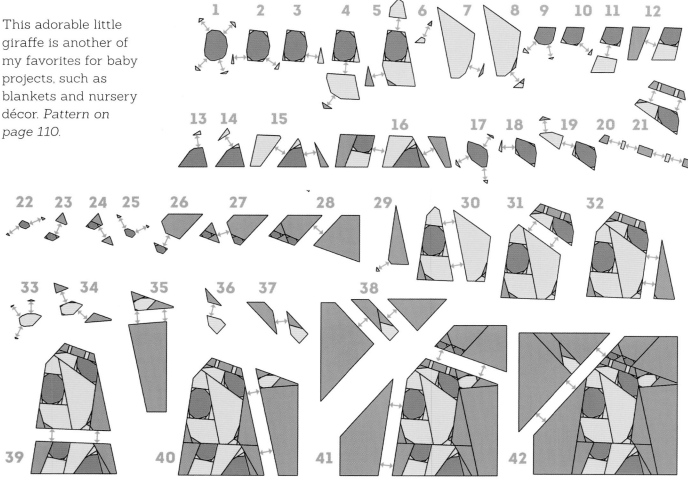

Zebra Foal

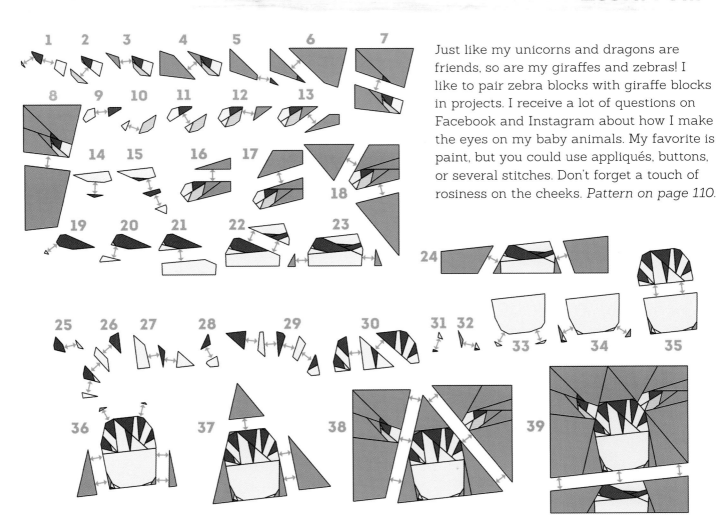

Just like my unicorns and dragons are friends, so are my giraffes and zebras! I like to pair zebra blocks with giraffe blocks in projects. I receive a lot of questions on Facebook and Instagram about how I make the eyes on my baby animals. My favorite is paint, but you could use appliqués, buttons, or several stitches. Don't forget a touch of rosiness on the cheeks. *Pattern on page 110.*

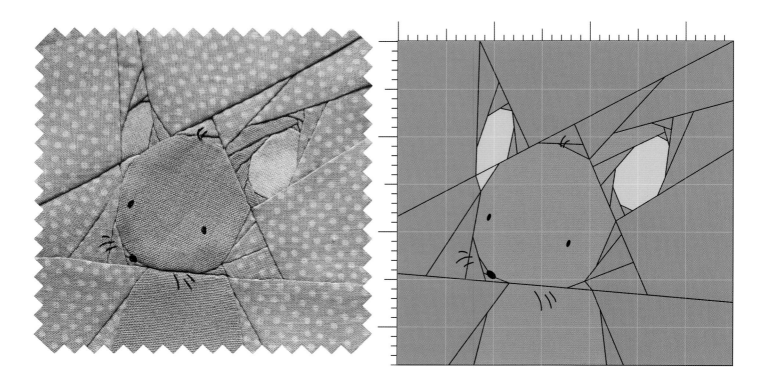

Baby Mouse

This shy and sweet baby mouse is one of my favorites. Try different pastel colors and decorative details, for example, a tiny button or bead for the nose. *Pattern on page 111.*

Panda Cub

I created this fluffy and soft baby panda especially for my fitness trainer. I had so much fun sewing the face. A child would love to see this friendly panda on a quilt, don't you think? *Pattern on page 111.*

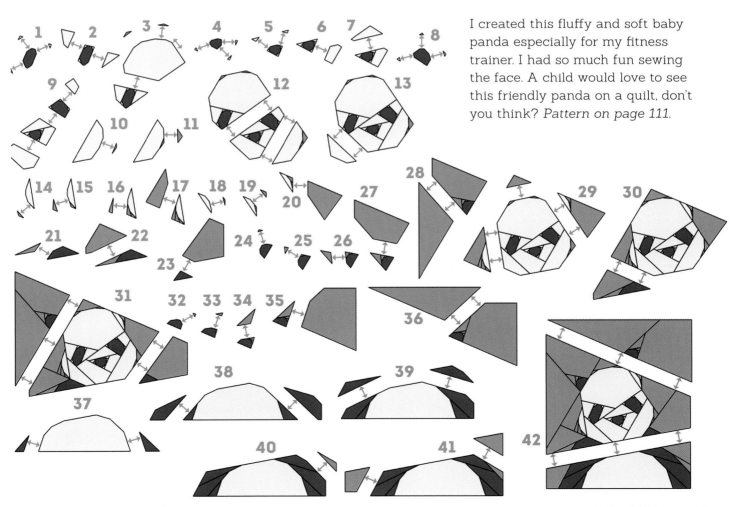

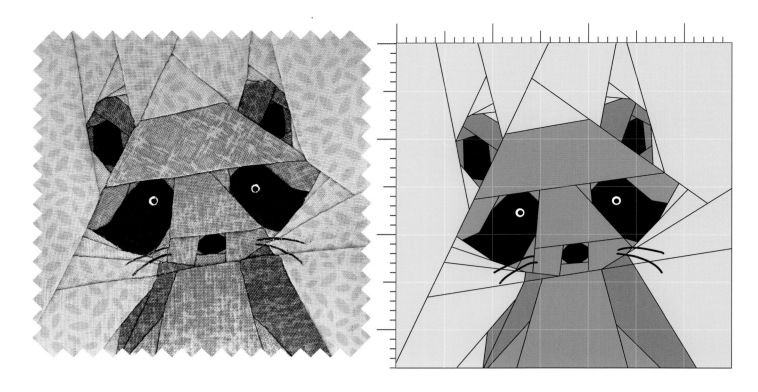

Raccoon Kit

When I want to cheer myself up, I like to watch funny animal videos, and I'm sure you know that there are many of them online! I found a smile and my inspiration for this block in a video about a baby raccoon and a cookie. This is an easy block to make. You can try different fabric combinations and tiny buttons or beads for the eyes. *Pattern on page 111.*

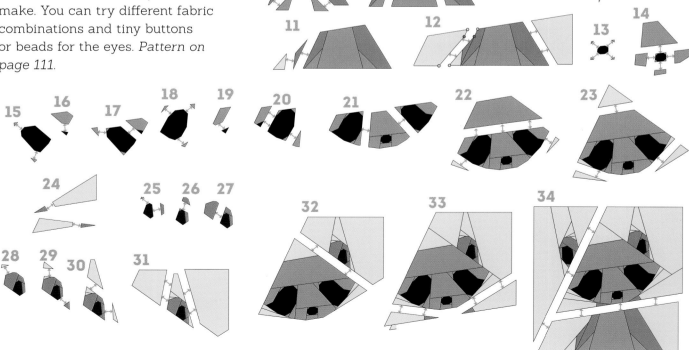

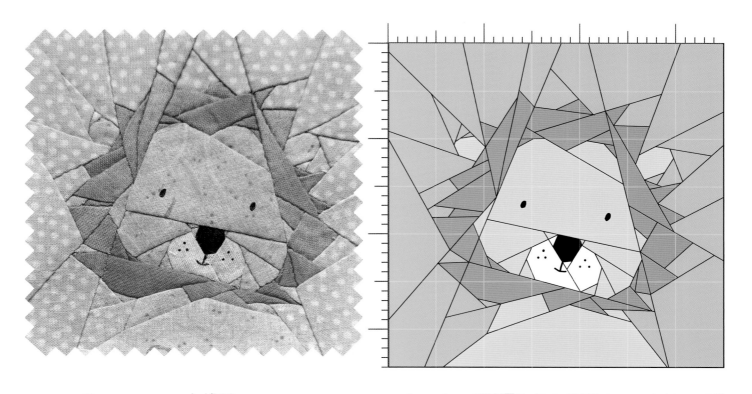

Lion Cub

This is one of my favorite baby animal blocks. The yellow and orange fabrics make it so bright and colorful! The pieces of the mane take some time to sew correctly, but the result is striking. *Pattern on page 111.*

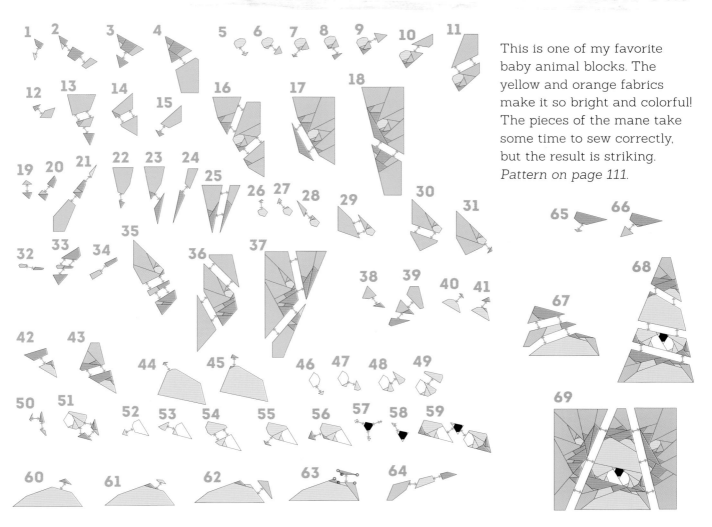

Patterns

Patterns shown at actual size. For practice, make one or more blocks at a larger size before trying them at actual size.

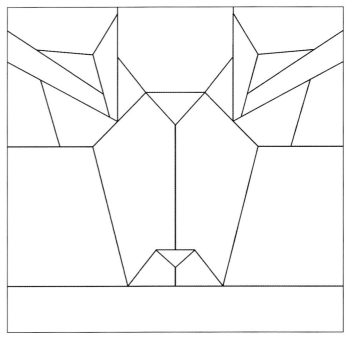

The Red-Nosed Reindeer, page 21

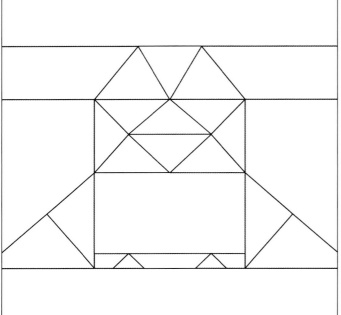

Happy Penguin, page 20

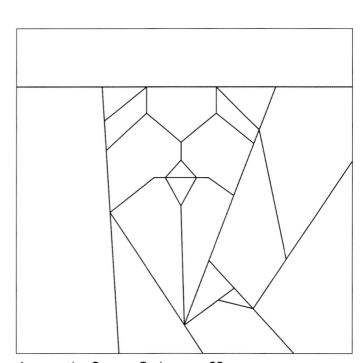

Aurora the Snowy Owl, page 23

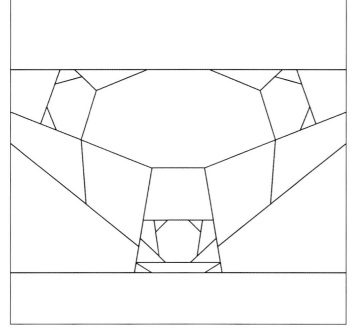

Serious Polar Bear, page 22

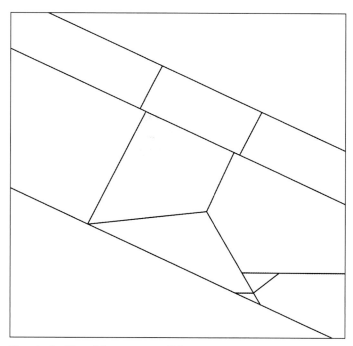

Santa's Stocking, page 24

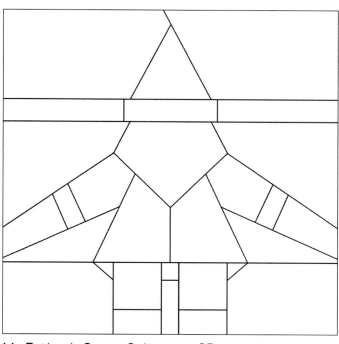

My Father's Santa Suit, page 25

Clever Santa, page 26

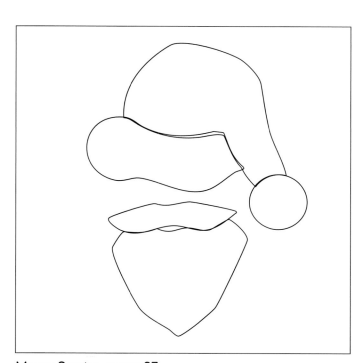

Merry Santa, page 27

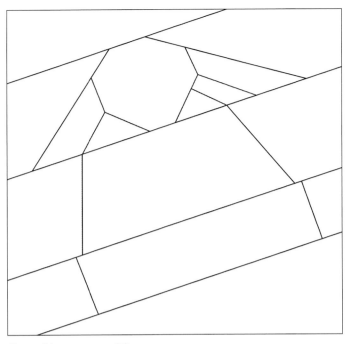

Cozy Hat, page 28

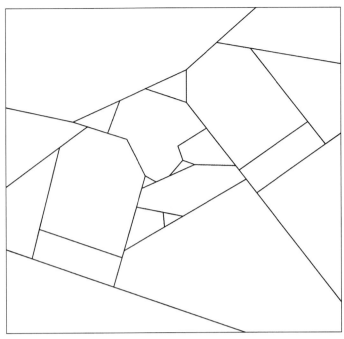

Warm Mittens, page 29

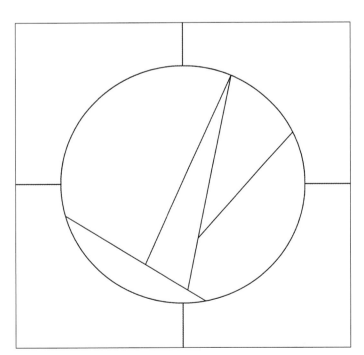

Ball Ornament, page 30

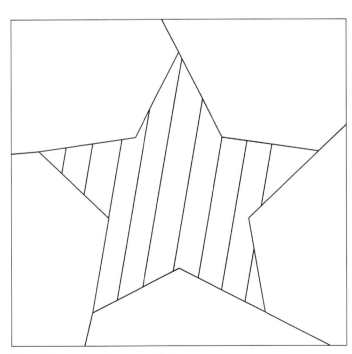

Star Ornament, page 31

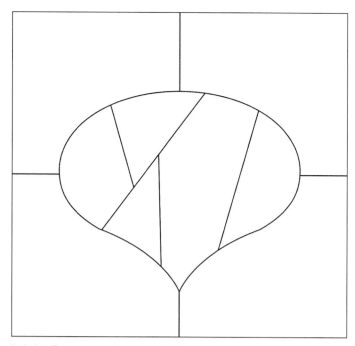

Icicle Ornament, page 32

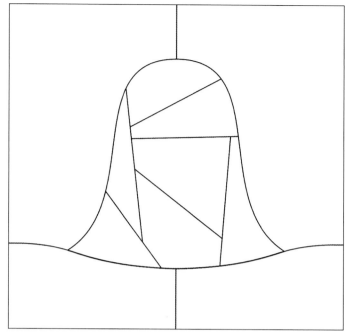

Bell Ornament, page 33

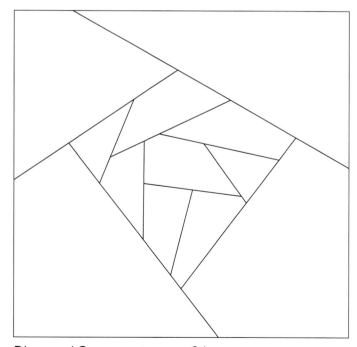

Diamond Ornament, page 34

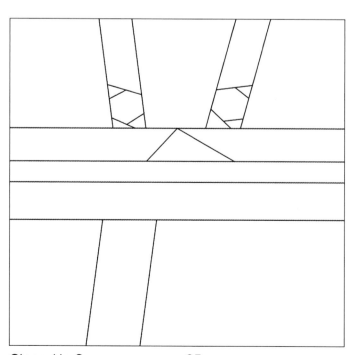

Close-Up Snowman, page 35

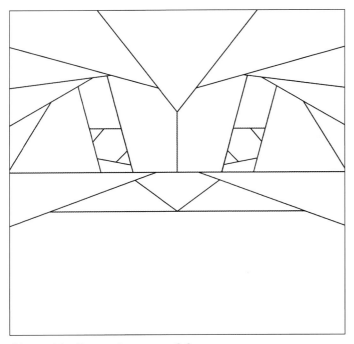

Close-Up Penguin, page 36

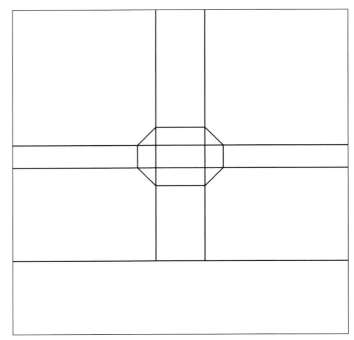

Santa's Belt, page 37

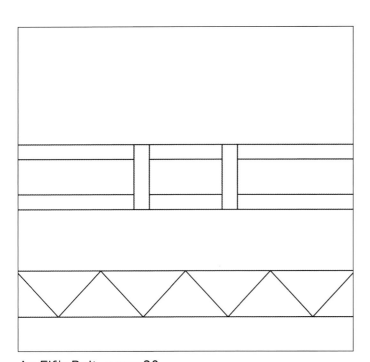

An Elf's Belt, page 38

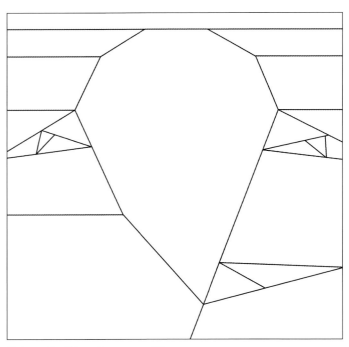

Friendly Ghost, page 42

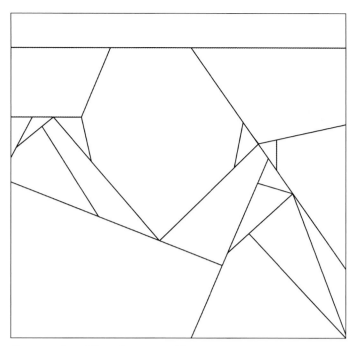

Screaming Ghost, page 43

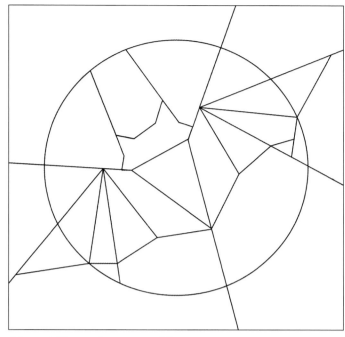

Almost Dracula, page 44

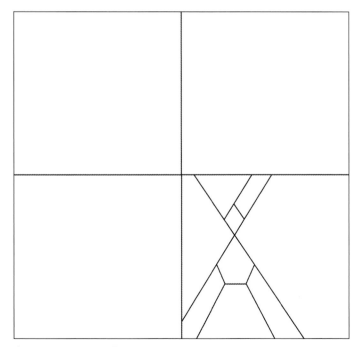

Spider, page 45

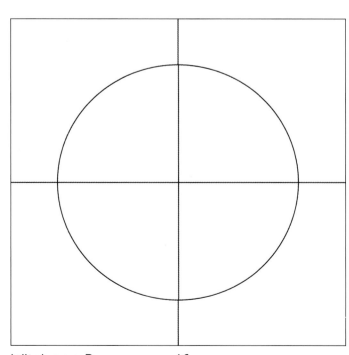

Witch on a Broom, page 46

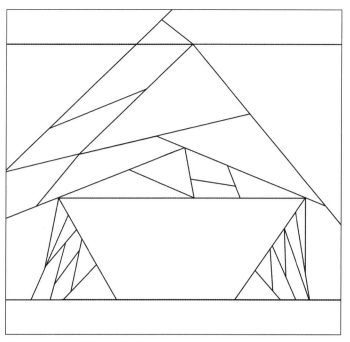

Redheaded Good Witch, page 47

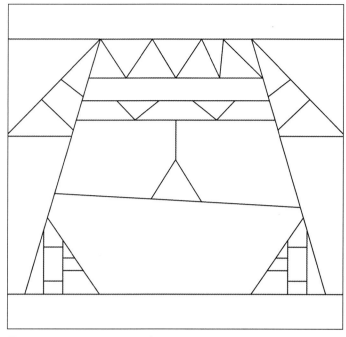

Frankenstein, page 48

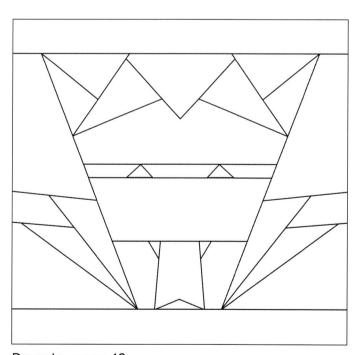

Dracula, page 49

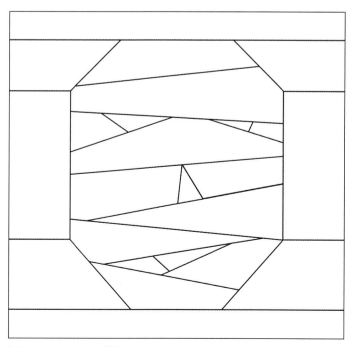

Mummy, page 50

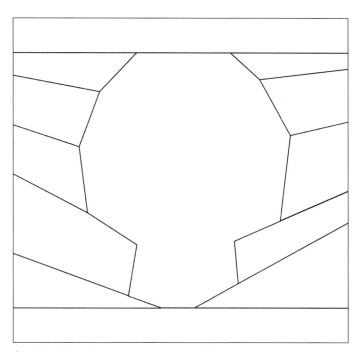

Skull with a Mustache, page 51

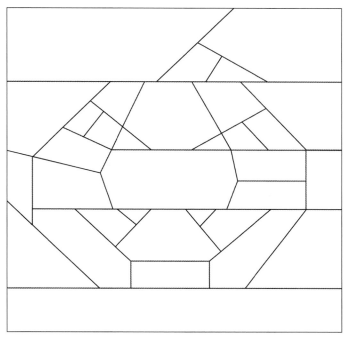

Spooky Pumpkin, page 52

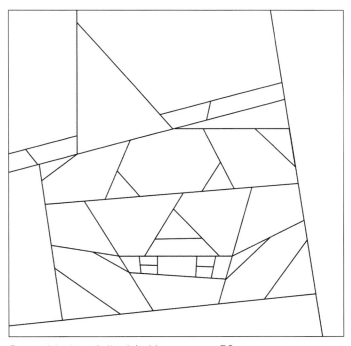

Pumpkin in a Witch's Hat, page 53

Smiling Pumpkin, page 54

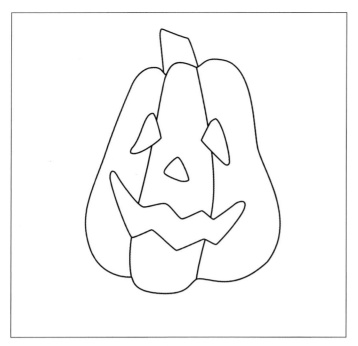

Scary Pumpkin, page 55

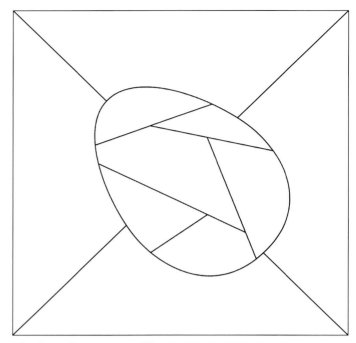

Modern Egg, page 58

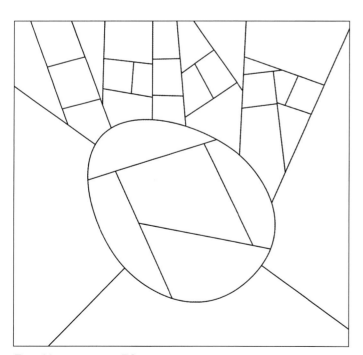

Egg Hunt, page 59

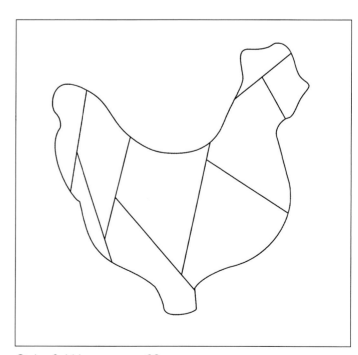

Colorful Hen, page 60

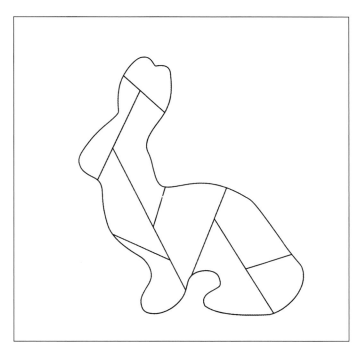

Rabbit Silhouette, page 61

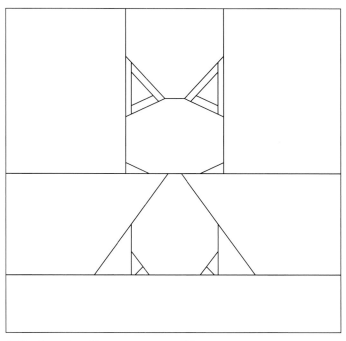

Otis the Gentleman, page 64

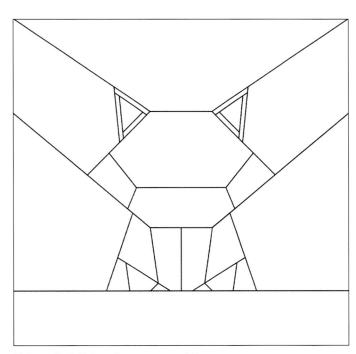

Friendly White Cat, page 65

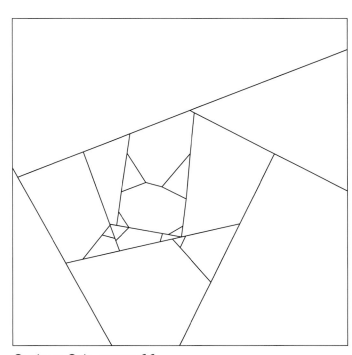

Curious Otis, page 66

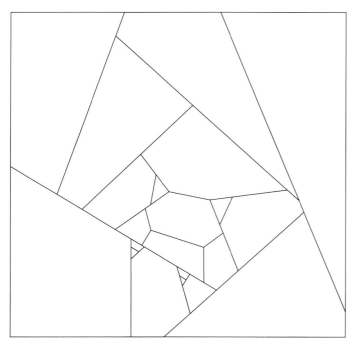

Peaceful Lily, page 67

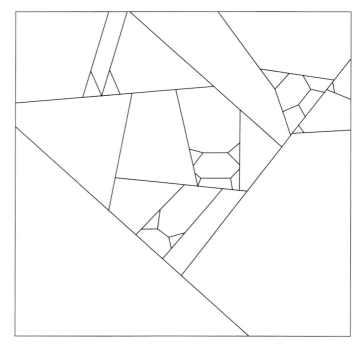

Little Kittens, page 68

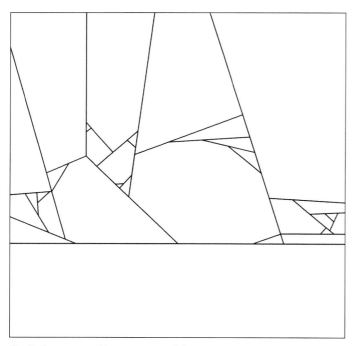

Soft Summer Nap, page 69

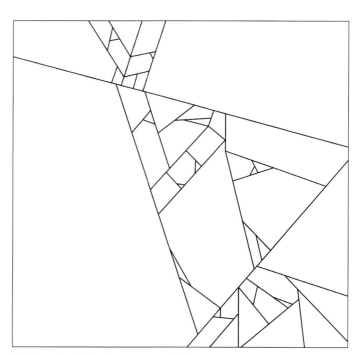

Butterfly Catcher, page 70

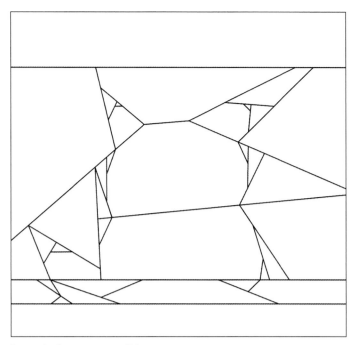

Lunchtime, page 71

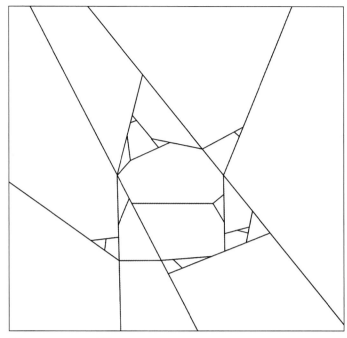

Siesta, page 72

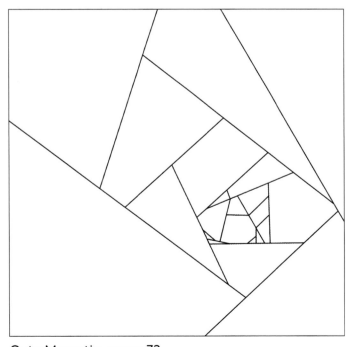

Cute Meowtie, page 73

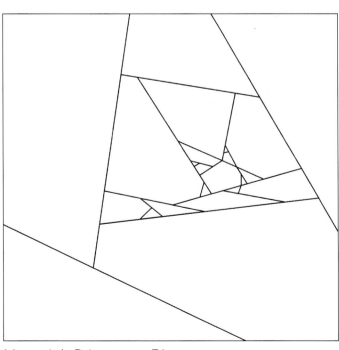

Meowtie's Prize, page 74

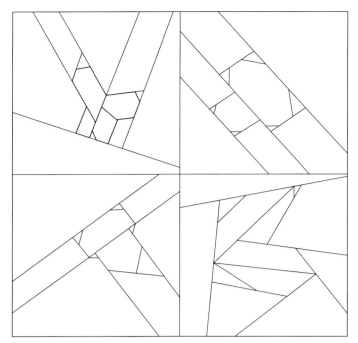

Forest Petites, page 75

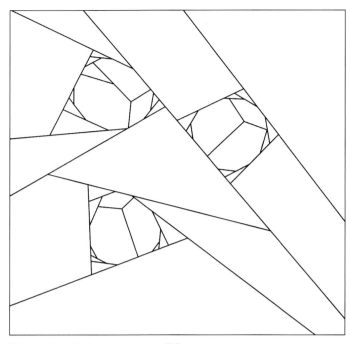

Forest Ladybugs, page 76

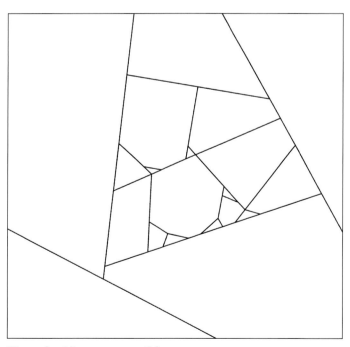

Time for Yoga, page 80

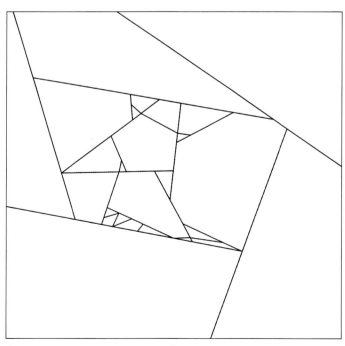

Soprano Is Awake, page 81

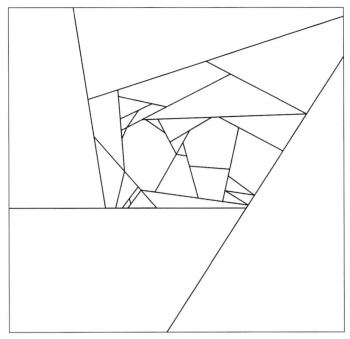

Cat Pose, page 82

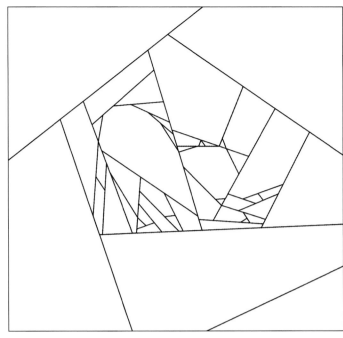

Puppy Pose, page 83

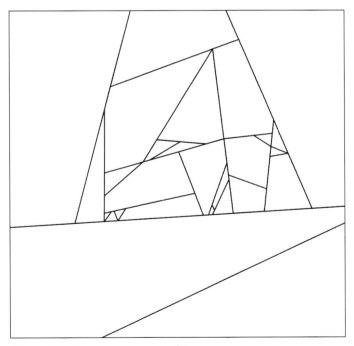

Planking Soprano, page 84

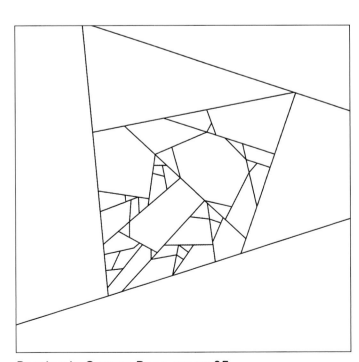

Resting in Corpse Pose, page 85

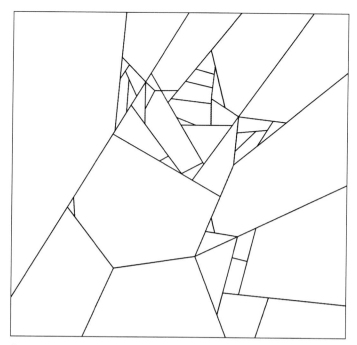

Baby Unicorn, page 88

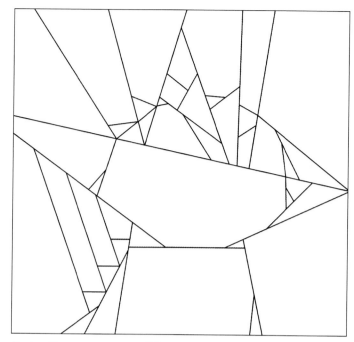

Baby Dragon, page 89

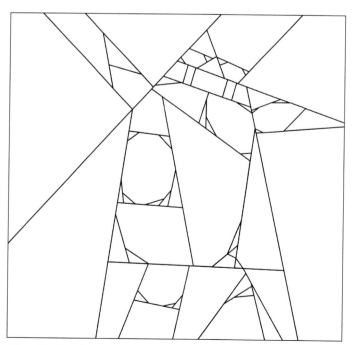

Giraffe Calf, page 90

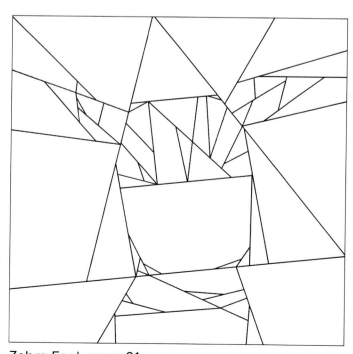

Zebra Foal, page 91

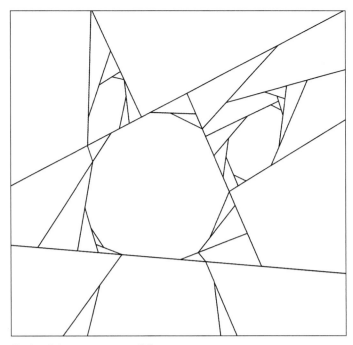

Baby Mouse, page 92

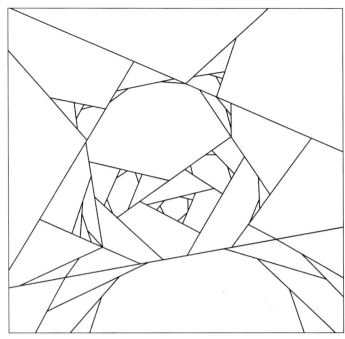

Panda Cub, page 93

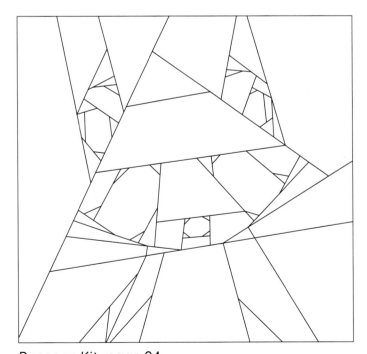

Raccoon Kit, page 94

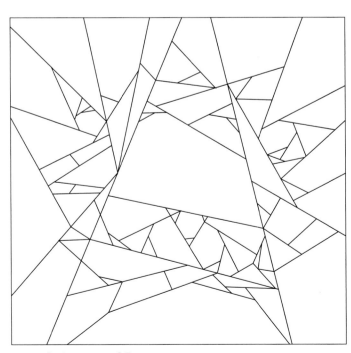

Lion Cub, page 95

Acknowledgments

Many thanks to my husband Nazar and my daughter Anastasiya, who inspire me every day of my life, who were very patient with me, and who shared all of my challenge days!

I would also like to thank Anastasiya Cherkis for her magical vision through the camera lens, Olga Chumakova for her work and optimism, all of my Instagram followers for their outstanding support and love, and Joy Paolozza for being my quilting godmother.

About the Author and Contributors

Olesya Lebedenko, Author

Author **Olesya Lebedenko** is an artist from Ukraine living in Canada, where she works and creates modern pattern designs. She is a teacher, designer, quilter, doll maker, author, magazine contributor, and entrepreneur as the founder and owner of Olesya Lebedenko Design. Her work has been featured in Canadian and Ukrainian publications, she has written countless tutorials and articles, and she has led hundreds of workshops all over Europe and Canada.

Olesya is a professional member of the International Quilt Association and the Canadian Quilters' Association. She is also a member of the York Heritage Quilters Guild, based in Toronto, as well as the Global Doll Society. To learn more about Olesya Lebedenko and to view her work, visit her website (*www.olesya-l-design.com*), her Instagram (*@olesyalebedenkodesign*), and her Etsy shop (*www.etsy.com/shop/OlesyaLebedenkoDsgn*).

Anastasya Cherkis, Photographer

Professional photographer **Anastasiya Cherkis** sees the whole world through the lens of her camera. This mom of three also loves nature, sports, and finding the harmony and beauty in life.

Olga Chumakova, Diagram Designer

As the creator of the step-by-step diagrams in this book, graphic designer **Olga Chumakova** knows how to make gorgeous order out of creative chaos. She's a happy mom and wife who is full of ideas, patience, and love.

The following images courtesy of Shutterstock.com:
wood background on cover, pages 1-5, 10-17, and project headings, Titus Group; page 9 (top), Lubava; page 11 (top), Lasmane; page 13 (bottom right), Seregam